VICTIMS OF CRIME

Their Rights and Human Rights

VICTIMS OF CRIME

Their Rights and Human Rights

CHANDRA SEN PRATAP SINGH
Law School, Banaras Hindu University
Varanasi.

Foreword by

DR. ANIRUDH PRASAD
Visiting Professor and Dean, Academic
Hidayatullah National Law University
Raipur—Chhattisgarh.

DEEP & DEEP PUBLICATIONS PVT. LTD.
F-159, Rajouri Garden, New Delhi-110027

VICTIMS OF CRIME

ISBN 978-81-8450-294-7

Typeset by S.S. COMPOSERS
3190, Mohindra Park, Shakur Basti, Delhi-110034.

Printed in India at MAYUR ENTERPRISES
WZ Plot No. 3, Gujjar Market, Tihar Village, New Delhi-110018.

Published by DEEP & DEEP PUBLICATIONS PVT. LTD.
F-159, Rajouri Garden, New Delhi-110027.
Phones: 25435369, 25440916
E-mail: ddpbooks@yahoo.co.in • ddpubs@gmail.com
Showroom:
2/13, Ansari Road, Daryaganj, New Delhi-110002 • Telefax: 23245122

Contents

Foreword

Justice is what Justice does. It is not cloistered virtue. It is a bond which holds society together. Administration of criminal justice through law aims at to standardize human behaviour and conduct to the extent necessary to maintain a desired level of individual freedom, safety and social order. Law is an instrument to ensure justice to all. It is one of the linking pins that hold the various components of criminal justice together as a cohesive order. Criminal law presents a framework around which the edifice of justice system is erected and maintained. It has also to balance the conflicting interests and ensure security of persons and property. Justice has to ensure fair deal and treatment of all. It has a protean face.

Victim's right was secured as private enterprise in early age. It was settled as a private matter. With a view to avoid blood feud the state tended to provide a framework in law for victims to pursue compensation for injuries through courts. Offenders could redeem themselves through the payment of compensation. It was known as *bot* or *wergild.*[1] However the system underwent seismic shift during the Middle Ages and state grasped and usurped the role of the victim. The civil liability was converted into criminal liability and there was clear shift from local to centralised law.[2] In

---

1. See Pollock, F. and Mitland, F., The History of English Law, Vol. 2, 2nd edn. (Cambridge University Press), 1898.
2. Coak, Jonathan, 'Victims' Rights, Human Rights and Criminal Justice —Reconceiving the Role of Third Parties', Oxford and Portland, Oregan (Hart Publishing), 2008, p. 2.

words of Ashworth, the transition probably owed "less to doctrinal legal distinction than to the usefulness of criminal jurisdiction as a source of funds for the Crown ...... and to the social significance of the administration of Criminal Justice as a mark of royal authority."[3] It was also so as criminal law began to be recognized as a useful tool for the state to regulate the behaviour of the citizens with a view to promote peace and the security of the nation. The shift also made private law affair the public law enforceable by law. Still victim had important role to play as initiator and late twelfth and early thirteenth century was marked by victim's private action through the "appeal of felony." The victim was restituted the loss suffered. That is reason why Schafer was prompted to describe the Middle Ages era as "the golden age of the victim."[4]

A shift took place and victim's role got minimized and crimes could be prosecuted through 'presentment' even without the victim's appeal.[5] The policy behind the administration of criminal justice began to be heavily influenced by the great Italian Criminologist Beccaria who propagated utilitarian view making victim's interest subservient to those of the interest of the society and believed that the role the criminal justice system was to subserve the interest of the society as a whole as opposed to providing redress for victims as on individualistic basis.[6]

This shift in outlook pushed victim aside. The tendency prompted Michael Fooner to comment, "the History of crime and punishment in the whole civilized world reveals a steadily increasing concern with the treatment of the criminal and actual blackout of the attention to the situation of the victim for more than 1000 years prior to the mid-twentieth century the victim of crime in our society and in the

3. Ashworth, A., "Punishment and Compensation: Victims, Offenders and the State", 6, *Oxford Journal of Legal Studies*, p. 86 (1986).
4. Schafer, The Victim and his Criminal (New York, Random House) p. 7 (1968).
5. *Supra*, n. 2, p. 3.
6. *Ibid.*, p. 5.

administration of justice has been ignored."[7] The poor victims of crime got completely ignored and overlook and misplaced sympathy for criminals aroused. This deficiency in criminal administration of justice was very aptly exposed by Mr. Justice V.R. Krishna Iyer in his judicial as well as extra judicial pronouncements. In his article contributed to *Indian Journal of Criminology* under caption, "The Criminal Process and Legal Aid", the learned judge asked, "tears shed for the accused are traditional and trendy but has the law none for the victim of crime, the unknown martyr?"

In the process of the administration of criminal justice victim became a 'forgotten man'. With emergence of reformatory theory and crime as a result of mental illness and human right approach toward offender the result is that a guilty man is lodged fed, clothed and entertained in a model cell at the expense of the state. Prison reform movement made criminality a privileged enterprise. Accused enjoy right to equality and equal protection of laws, right against *ex-post facto* laws, protection against double jeopardy, protection against self-incrimination, right to have freedom from unwarranted arrest, right to legal aid and defence, right to speedy trial, right to live with human dignity, protection against unwarranted handcuffing. The situation led Mr. Justice V.R. Krishna Iyer to expose the inherent weakness in the system. The learned judge observed: "it is a weakness of our jurisprudence that victims of crime and the distress of the dependents of the victim do not attract attention of law. In fact, the victim reparation is still the vanishing point of our criminal law. This is the deficiency in the system, which must be rectified by the legislature."[8]

In first phase of human rights enthroning on international scene through the Universal Declaration of Human Rights (1948), and International Covenant on Civil and Political Rights (1966) gave new impetus to human rights of prisoners. The added dimension reached its height through

7. Science, Vol. 153, No. 3740, Sept. 2 (1966), see also Mahmood Bin Muhammad, 'The Victim in Criminal Justice' (in) S. Venugopal Rao (ed.) Perspectives in Criminology, pp. 213-28.
8. Rattan Singh *v.* State of Punjab (1979) 4 SCC 719.

dynamic and liberal interpretation of Article 21 and expanding the meaning of life and personal liberty.[9] The Supreme Court became too much conscious of rendering justice to prisoners and in *Rammurthy* v. *State of Karnataka*[10] it did not consider overcrowding in jail *per se* as unconstitutional, but held that "there is no doubt that the same does not affect the health of prisoners. The same very adversely affects hygienic conditions." The pro-prisoner reformative outlook speaks of the correctional philosophy to include—(1) Prison is no more considered as a 'House of Captives' but a correctional institution; (2) a person coming to Jail does not become a non-person; (3) prisoners have all constitutional rights except those limited by imprisonment; (4) human rights are a basic element of correctional justice assumptions that hate the crime, not the criminal; (5) a prisoner should have human rights in order to learn to respect the human rights of others; (6) debarring a prisoner from human rights would pose a direct threat to our own humanity and civilization; (7) prison regime help prisoners to lead law-abiding, self-supporting, reformed and socially rehabilitated life. As Mr. Justice V.R. Krishna Iyer enumerated in *Sunil Batra (I)* v. *Delhi Administration*[11] human rights initiatives in prison are based on three principles, viz., maintaining human dignity, rights of prisoners and needs of special categories of prisoners like, women, juveniles and under-trials.

It goes without saying that Anglo-Saxon-adversial pattern ignored the victims. For a long time it has been forgotten that victims too should be endowed with human rights. When victims' right is given due place some sort of

9. Protection against torture in the prison (Sunil Batra *v.* Delhi Administration, A.I.R. 1978 S.C. 1976); right not to be put in solitary confinement (Sunil Batra (No. 2) *v.* Delhi Administration, A.I.R. 1980 S.C. 1579); right to meet friends, relatives, media persons and lawyers (M.H. Hoskot *v.* State of Maharashtra, A.I.R. 1978 S.C. 1548); free legal Aid and assistance (Hoskot's case); right to speedy trial (Hussainara Khatoon (No. 1) *v.* Home Secretary, State of Bihar, A.I.R. 1982 S.C. 1167); right against handcuffing (Prem Shankar *v.* Delhi Administration, A.I.R. 1980 S.C. 1535).
10. 1997 Cr. L.J. 1508 (S.C.).
11. (1978) 4 S.C.C. 494.

conflict of interests would be unavoidable. As Garland points out "a zero-sum policy game is assumed wherein the offender's gain is the victim's loss, and being "for" victims automatically means being tough on offenders.[12] Anyway, human rights approach also started victim-oriented initiatives. It also views as fulfiling service rights."[13] Victims' rights approach or victims' participation model are better ensured under inquisitorial system where victim has better control over the procedure. Victims' interests are better protected through recognition of victims' rights. Human right of victim is viewed in light of his 'right to justice'. International human rights law enunciated in Article 8 of the Universal Declaration of Human Rights, 1948 notes that "everyone has the right to effective remedy by the competent national tribunals for acts violating the fundamental rights granted to him by the Constitution or by law." Article 2(3) of the International Covenant on Civil and Political Rights requires states to ensure the effective enforcement of freedoms and Article 14 of the Convention Against Torture specifies that States must ensure that victims are able to take legal action for 'an enforceable right to fair and adequate compensation'. Article 7 of International Covenant on Civil and Political Rights read with Article 2 ensures that "those found guilty must be held responsible, and the alleged victims must themselves have effective remedies at their disposal including the right to obtain compensation."[14] Victims' rights may include the following:

(I) A Right to Truth

A core interest of the victim is that the truth be revealed and an appropriate disposition be reached.[15] In

---

12. Garland, D. The Culture of Control (Oxford Univ. Press), 2001, Ch. I, Roach, K., Due Process and Victim's Rights (Univ. of Toronto Press, 1999) Ch. I.
13. Ashworth, Victims' Impact Statements and Sentencing (1993) *Criminal Law Review,* 498.
14. 37 UNGAOR Supp. (No. 40) at 94, UN Doc. No. A/37/40 1982.
15. Beloof, D., The Third Model of Criminal Process: The Victim Participation Model (1999) 2, *Utah Law Review,* 289.

words of former U.N. Special Rapporteur, Theo Von Proven: "only the complete and public revelation of the truth will make it possible to satisfy the basic requirements of the principles of justice."[16]

Right to truth involves right to information. Council of Europe outlines its commitment to "ensure that victims have access to information of relevance to their case and necessary for the protection of their interests and the exercise of their rights."[17] Similar is the provision under Victims' Declaration at U.N. Platform in 1985. Thus, victim has right to know. At state level Jerome Frank is of view that the 'right' theory has invaluable quality of searching truth. To quote him "... Macaulay said that we obtain the fairest decision 'when two men argue, as fairly as possible, on opposite sides' for then it is certain that no important consideration will altogether escape notice."[18]

(2) The Right to Reparation

Victims' right to reparation is most venerable and most central of legal principles.[19] Reparation comes from the root 'repair' aims to rectify harm caused to the victim and restore his earlier position. It connotes the idea of compensational 'damages', restitution or 'restoration' is used interchangeably.

At international level the provisions were made in the Hague Conventions of 1899 and 1907 and they were affirmed in Factory at Chorzow case in 1928 by the I.C.J.[20] It pointed out that "reparation must, as far as possible, wipe out all the consequences of the illegal act and reestablish the situation

---

16. Van Boven, T. (1993). The Right to Restitution, Compensation and Rehabilitation for Victims of Gross Violations of Human Rights and Fundamental Freedoms (UN Doc. E/CN.4/SUB.3/1993/8) (Geneva: U.N.).
17. Rec. (2006) 8(6).
18. Frank, J., Courts on Trial: Myth and Reality of American Justice (Princeton, Princeton Univ. Press) 1949, p. 49.
19. Roht-Arriaza, Punishment, Redress and Pardon: Theoretical and Psychological Approaches in N. Roht-Arriaza (ed.) *Impurity and Human Rights in International Law and Practice* (USA Oxf. Univ. Press) p. 13 (1995).
20. Series A., No. 17 (1927) PCIJ No. 8.

which would in all probability, have existed if that act had not been committed."[21]

The idea of reparation has found place in human rights law. The international law principle of state responsibility got converted into human rights law liability. Human rights treaties have created directly accessible rights for individual victims.[22] Several international bodies have preferred victim-oriented perspective keeping in view the needs and rights of victims.[23] Similar approach has been adopted by European Convention on Human Rights. Article 41 requires 'just satisfaction to the injured party. In *Velasquez Rodriguez*,[24] the Inter-American Court accepted duty to make adequate reparation for violation of international obligation. It spoke of fair compensation to victim and explained reparation to entail, "the restoration of the prior situation, the reparation of the consequences of the violation, and the indemnification of patrimonial and non-patrimonial damages including emotional harm."[25] European Convention on Compensation of Victims of Violent Crimes recognizes victim or in case of his death due to crime of violence, his dependent's right to receive compensation. Article 2 speaks of State compensation if compensation is not fully available from other sources. In the case of intentional violence State has to compensate irrespective of offender being prosecuted or not. Thus, burden in the first place rests with the offender rather than on the State. If offender is unable to compensate then it may shift to State. State may be relieved of responsibility in three situations: (1) on account of the victims' conduct before, during or after the crime; (2) on account of the victims' involvement in organized crime, or (3) if a full award is

---

21. *Ibid.*, p. 21.
22. Doak, Jonathan, Victims' Rights, Human Rights and Criminal Justice, 2008, p. 212.
23. Basic Principles and Guidelines on the Rights to a Remedy and Reparation for Victims of Violations of International Human Rights and Humanitarian Law, Report of Commission on Human Rights, 2005 and Resolution of General Assembly, Dec., 2005.
24. (1989) 28ILM 291.
25. *Ibid.* at (26).

contrary to a sense of justice or public policy. European Council requires signatories to take appropriate measures to encourage the offender to provide adequate compensation to victims.[26] Some scholars have treated reparation more than restitution. To quote Zedner—

> "..........Reparation should ordinarily connote a wider set of aims. It involves more than 'making good' the damage done to property, body or psyche. It must entail recognition of the harm done to the social relationship between offender and victim and the damage done to the victim's social rights in his or her property or person."[27]

In 1964 in England a method was evolved to compensate innocent victims of violence and an expression of social sympathy towards victims.[28] It was based on expectation rather than legally enforceable right.[29] Compensation is governed by Criminal Injuries Compensation Act, 1955. It is well thought that reparation should come from offender. In case of unidentified offender or lack of means with offender to compensate victim, state should bear responsibility.

The movement for victim-oriented criminal law jurisprudence has reinforced five-fold basic critique of the criminal justice system:

1. That criminal justice personnel—the police, prosecutors, defence attorneys, judges, probation officers, parole boards ... were systematically over-looking or neglecting the legitimate needs of crime victims until they all began their campaign;

---

26. EU Framework Decision, Article (2).
27. Zedner, L. (1994), Reparation and Retribution. Are they Reconcilable? 57, *Modern Law Review*, 228.
28. Goodey, J. (2005), Victim and Victimology: Research, Policy and Practice (Harlow, Pearson Longman), p. 141.
29. *Ibid.*, p. 142.

2. That there was a prevailing tendency on the part of the public as well as agency officials to impairly blame victims for facilitating or even provoking crimes;
3. That explicit standards of fair treatment were required to protect the interests of complainants and prosecution witnesses...;
4. That people who suffered injuries ... ought to receive reimbursement ...; and
5. That the best way to make sure that victims could pursue their personal goals and protect their own best interest was by granting them formal rights within the criminal justice system.[30]

Contemporary criminal justice policy conferring new legal rights upon victims puts emphasis of 'social rights' or 'service rights'. With enactment of Human Rights Act, 1998 in U.K. victims have been given certain substantive and procedural rights. White Paper issued on *Justice for All in 2002* promised to "rebalance the criminal justice system in favour of the victim and the community so as to reduce crime and bring more offenders to justice."[31]

New consciousness—human rights dimension of victims' right has added many problems. *First,* it has to dwindle between the Scylla of neglect of the victims of crimes and charybdis of the violation of accused's protection. There was much truth and sincerity in declaration of U.S. President's Task Force on Victims of Crime when it said, "the innocent victim of crime have been overlooked, their pleas for justice have gone unheeded, and their wounds—personal emotional, and financial—have gone unattended."[32] This provides for positive and creative thinking towards

30. Karmen, A. (1992), Who's Against Victims' Rights? *8, St. John's Journal of Legal Commentary, 157.*
31. Home Office (2002a) para 0.3.
32. President's Task Force on Victims of Crime, Final Report (Government Printing Office, Washington D.C., 1982); see also Canadian Federal-Provincial Task Force on Justice for Victims of Crime, 1983.

victimology and victims' rights. It generates the idea of victims' right as recognition of dignity and reduction of the chances of the secondary victimization of victims. But the U.S. experience has put the danger of victims' movement being hi-jacked[33] and too much emphasis on victims' right would lead to justify the proverb—to rob Peter the offender to pay for services for Paul the victim.[34] and there are chances of the erosion of offender's right and they may be subjected to positive segregation. It is wise to avoid zero-sum game.[35] *Secondly,* reparation right communicates the notion—to have harm made good. It is itself not beyond suspicion. Can victims be made to feel always good after experiencing torture, humiliation and loss of prestige in society? How reparation will ensure justice and good to rape victims? In addition, the chief goal of criminal justice has a societal dimension and the goal is punishment rather than reparation. Furthermore, notions of satisfaction, 'truth' and 'guarantee of non-repetition' are not very much in tune with adversial system.[36] *Thirdly,* there is some controversy as to the effectiveness of the victim's lawyer and ultimate duty cast on prosecutor and judge to safeguard the victim's interest has to be performed. On the other hand, victim's active participation is discouraged by the reluctance of the legal profession to advise them of their rights and push forward their interests proactively.[37] The reason behind it is that—"judges and prosecutor still regard the victim predominantly in his or her role as a witness, whereas the victim wants to be regarded as party to the proceedings."[38] *Fourthly,* there is limit of

---

33. Elias, R., Victim Still: The Political Manipulation of Crime Victims (Sage, Newbury Park Cal.), 1993.
34. Williams, B., "The Victim's Charter: Citizens as Consumers of Criminal Justice Services" (1999) 38, *Howard Journal of Criminal Justice,* 384.
35. For Critical Study on the point see, Doak, Jonathan, Victims' Rights, Human Rights and Criminal Justice, 2008, pp. 246-49.
36. *Ibid.,* p. 253.
37. *Ibid.,* p. 272.
38. Kury, Hand Kaiser, M. (1991): The Victim's Position Within The Criminal Proceedings—An Empirical Study (in) Kaiser G. and Teske Jr. (1994). The Position of Victim in Criminal Procedure—Results of a German Study, 3, *International Review of Victimology,* 69.

restorative justice which requires face-to-face or indirect dealing between victims and offenders. This is clear from the well known definition of Marshall—"Restorative justice is a process whereby all the parties with a stake in a particular offence come together to resolve and its implications for the future."[39] The interest primarily are psychological or emotional in nature.[40] The problem may be realized where offenders are not caught and there would be no body to "come to terms." Again there may be problem in cases of corporate victimization like shop theft, burglary or vandalisation of commercial premises. In such cases losses are covered by insurance.[41] *Fifthly*, restorative justice has a tone of active participation by offender and victim in the process. As the United Nations has put in this process "the offender and/ or any other individuals or community members affected by a crime participate actively together in the resolution of matters arising from the crime."[42] But in situation of non-participating victim there may be problem. A research conducted keeping two types of victims focused initiative—One Stop Shop (OSS) keeping victims informed about the progress of their case and Victims' Statements (V.S.) providing victims with the opportunity to describe the impact of the crime upon them including psychological, financial, physical and emotional impact, concluded that, "schemes that provide information to victims without interaction and discussion with them do not in themselves increase satisfaction with the criminal justice process."[43] *Sixthly*, human rights dimension has enormously increased the definition of victim. The President's Crime Commission Report, 1967 says

---

39. Marshall, T., The Evolution of Restorative Justice in Britain (1996), 4, *European Journal on Criminal Policy and Research,* 21 (at p. 37).
40. Zehr, H., Changing Lenses: A New Focus for Crime and Justice (Herald Press, Scotesdale Penn, 1990) 32.
41. Hoyle, Carolyn and Young, Richard (ed.) New Visions of Crime Victims, 2002, Chap. 6, pp. 133-72.
42. U.N. Draft Declaration on Basic Principles on the use of Restorative Justice Programmes in Criminal Matters (United Nations, New York, NY, 1999).
43. Sanders, A., Hoyle, C. and Cape, E., Victim Impact Statements: Don't Work, Can't Work' (2001), *Criminal Law Review,* 447 at p. 452.

that; "Every American is, in a sense, a victim of crime, violence and theft have ....injured, often irreparably, hundreds of thousands of citizens."[44] The New Shorter Oxford English Dictionary defines the word victim in inclusive way to include, "a person killed or tortured by another; a person subjected to cruelty, oppression or other harsh, or unfair treatment, or suffering death, injury, ruin, etc., as a result of an event, circumstance, or oppressive or adverse important agency." New and new categories of victims, quite unknown earlier are copping up. Studies have started about the male victims of rape and possibility is being searched to discussed rape victims among homo-sexuals, gays, lesbians, transsexuals, bi-sexuals (LGBT).[45] Attempts have also been made to research on Female-on-Male Domestic Abuse instead of Traditional Male-on-Female Domestic Violence so as to expose that there are evidences that men and women are victimized in the home to broadly similar degrees.[46] *Seventhly*, there are certain inherent limitations attached with adversial justice in relation to protection, participation, justice and reparation meant to be secured for victims.[47] It does not provide sufficient protection in relation to secondary victimisation that occurs in the course of criminal trials. It does not allow participation of victim as the inquisitorial system allows. Attention is shifted from the goal of truth finding to the effectiveness of the games players.[48]

In backdrop of the preceding discussion the book authored by Mr. Chandra Sen Pratap Singh under caption "Victims of Crime: Their Rights and Human Rights" is most timely, promising, challenging and thought provoking. It is

44. The Challenge of Crime in a Free Society: A Report by the President's Commission on Law Enforcement and Administration of Justice (U.S. Government Printing Office, Washington, D.C., 1967).
45. Allen, Stephanie, "Male Victims of Rape. Responses to a Perceived Threat to Masculinity (in) Hoyle, Carolyn and Young, Richard (ed.) New Visions of Crime Victims, 2002, pp. 23-48.
46. Gardy, Ann, "Female-on-Male Domestic Abuse: Uncommon or Ignored? (in) Hoyle and Young, *Ibid.*, pp. 71-96.
47. Doak, Jonathan, *supra* f.n. 2, pp. 249-62.
48. *Id.*

bound to regenerate a new outlook and appreciation of multifacet problems faced by the victims with felt necessities of sensitivisation about victims in general and sex-victims in particular.

The book starts with introduction of radical international concern, changing judicial outlook and emerging interest in victimology. Chapter 2 presents the historical perspective of the role of victims experiencing golden time of medieval period to long journey as 'forgotten man', most neglected segment of administration of criminal justice and resurrection of victims' due place in dispensation of justice process. Chapter 3 exhaustively deals with different theories of justice putting main emphasis on restorative justice with a view to strengthen the victim-oriented criminal justice system. Chapter 4 of the study is rightly devoted to world-wide concern towards victims' rights as in the present age of globalisation no body can afford to avoid the impact of international and transnational developments in the field of realization of victims' rights in proper perspective. The author has given full account of efforts at national level in India safeguarding the interest of victims through compensatory justice under Cr.P.C., Probation of Offenders Act, Fatal Accidents Act, The Workmen's Compensation Act, Motor Vehicles Act, Public Liability Insurance Act, The National Environment Tribunal Act, Protection of Civil Rights Act, The S.Cs and S.Ts (Prevention of Atrocities) Act, etc. A live discussion is also presented on Malimath Committee Report in Chapter 5. The study in Chapter 6 deals with activist judicial role in awarding compensation to victims of illegal arrest and unwarranted detention, police atrocities, custodial deaths and fake encounters, police firing, riots and untoward happenings, rape, etc. The study reveals how judiciary has broken the traditional barrier of *locus standi* and awarding punishment and has evolved public interest litigation, interim relief by awarding compensation and final relief by awarding compensation for human rights violation and ordering prosecution of offender government servants. This has been done by ensuring public law remedy by enforcing a newly searched category constitutional tort. And at the end epilogue has concluded the study that once "forgotten man" has attracted the concern of national and international bodies. The author has rightly pointed out that in India victims of the crimes are more or less still forgotten men in the criminal justice system. The judiciary marches one step ahead and two steps backward. To be specific Supreme Court's progressive and pro-rape victim approach to award compensation and interim maintenance in *Bodhisattva Gautam's case*[49] could not have a long merry day. The author rightly exposes dichotomy between the legally fully safeguarded accused and not so well recognized rights of victims and says that "the need of hour in the country is to do away with inequity between a fully articulated system of procedural rights of the accused and virtually non-existent procedural rights of victims."[50]

The author has come with a number of valuable suggestions for amendments in substantive criminal law (I.P.C.) and the procedural law—Cr.P.C., Constitution of compensation fund to compensate the victims of crimes of different types and state responsibility in cases of unidentified offenders or inability of offender to compensate.

I strongly recommend the book and hope that it will prove its worth among students, teachers and all components of administration of justice.

DR. ANIRUDH PRASAD
Visiting Professor and Dean, Academic
Hidayatullah National Law University
Raipur—Chhattisgarh.

49. A.I.R. 1996 S.C. 922.
50. The Supreme Court and the Gujarat High Court took different views soon after the Bodhisattva case.

Preface

With the dawn of human rights movement, modern liberal democracy and welfare state a revolutionary change has come to the fore about the thinking and viewing of administration of criminal justice. This new approach gives due credence to all the components of crime, i.e. the offender, the society and the victim. Victim, once forgotten, has acquired certain status in administration of criminal justice and victims' right is becoming centre of attraction. This book under caption "Victims of Crime: Their Rights and Human Rights" is an attempt to focus the problem of victims of the crime who are forced to bear torture, humiliation and deprivation.

Rule of law aims to provide justice through the reign of law. Justice to all is the signature tune of our constitutional commitment. But in dealing with the issue in India as well as in other parts of the world, victims of crime had remained almost all neglected or 'forgotten men' since long. The violation of social norms inherently lies in the nature of the people. For a long time when individuals violated the norms, administration of criminal justice tried to enforce the rule of law curbing their violations, maintenance of law and order, conviction of the offender, reducing crime and rehabilitating the violators of law in society with the help of correction institutions. The approach was limited to criminological and penological perspective. The emphasis of the administration of the criminal justice was on the aphorism, "if every saint has a past, every sinner has a future." Victims of the crime remained overlooked, neglected and forgotten men.

The victim-oriented administration of criminal justice is of recent origin, although its seeds were lying in early times of civilization. The victim-oriented administration of criminal justice is inspired by victimology about which Mr. Justice V.R. Krishna Iyer has remarked that "victimology did not dawn one fine day but has been part of the Code of Hammurabi (Babylon) and has been hinted at in ancient texts, Greek, Roman and Indian." But it disappeared in historical perspective when state took the place of victim in prosecuting the offenders. With the emergence of the idea of victimology which was coined by Benjamin Mendelson human face of criminal justice came to be given the prominence. The primary object of the interest of victimology is the person of the victim. It is the science of victims. A new impetus was given in direction of the recognition of victim's right with the United Nations Declaration on the Basic Principles of Justice for Victims of Crime and Abuse of Power. The Declaration issued as Charter of Victim's Right in 1985.

The book, while introducing the subject of victimological interest, begins with the hypothesis that despite some provisions for providing restitutive and compensatory justice to the victims of crimes Indian legislative endeavour is not very much encouraging.

After giving a sketch of role of victims in administration of criminal justice in historical perspective the study shows that there has been march towards the victim-oriented criminal justice system which includes the distributive and corrective justice, civil and criminal justice giving the account of shifting paradigm from punitive justice to restorative justice. It clarifies the idea of restorative and compensatory justice with added dimension of assistance programmes for the victims.

The book also shows a world-wide trend towards realisation of the victims' rights. It includes redressal of victim's Grievances under United Nations Declaration, measures ensuring justice to the victims in common law countries and the civil law countries.

After giving the full account of and establishing the need as well as position of victims'-oriented administration of justice on world plane the study presents the position of restitutive, compensatory and assistance justice to the victims of crimes under statutory provisions in India, namely, Cr.P.C.

and some other statutes not technically falling under the criminal law scheme but providing for compensation and assistance to the victims. The study shows a tendency in Law Commission of India's report, Malimath Committee Report and other researches suggesting legislation on par with compensatory and restitutive method adopted in other countries of the world and notices lack of enthusiasm on the part of legislature in India. The present provisions are insufficient and ineffective, but legislature is not that much responsive as it should be.

Some progressive, responsive and victim-oriented administration of criminal justice is discernible from the creative and activist Judicial Role in awarding compensation to the victims as a public law remedy. The Judiciary has been more responsive to the victim's right both against the individual offenders and victims of oppression by the state officials. It has done justice to the victims by awarding compensation in cases of illegal arrest and unwarranted detention; cases of the victims of police atrocities, custodial deaths and fake encounters, cases of the victims of police firing, riots and untoward happenings and cases of the victims of rape. The Supreme Court has used writ jurisdiction in cases of the violation of life and liberty rights of the citizens both by the state and individuals. It has awarded interim compensation, allowed public interest petitions to safeguard the victims' rights and awarded compensation to rape victims irrespective nationality. The Supreme Court has issued directions in a number of cases to safeguard the rights of the victims which shows a healthy trend. But much is needed to be done.

The author is very much thankful to all teachers and colleagues who have helped and inspired in more than one way. The present book is modified and enlarged form of the author's dissertation submitted for award of LL.M. degree. The author is thankful to library staff of Allahabad University, D.D.U. Gorakhpur University and B.H.U.

The author owes a debt to Professor Anirudh Prasad which no word of gratitude will suffice. Both as a father and as a scholar of repute Prof. Prasad has been a constant source of inspiration. He has enormously helped and encouraged the author by adding Foreword to the book.

The author is also thankful to Mr. G.S. Bhatia who has brought the book in readable form in record time. The motto of the author has been "Let the noble thoughts come to us from all sides." Efforts have been made to make the book immune from blemishes, still suggestions are most welcome.

Varanasi C.S.P. SINGH

Abbreviations

A.I.R. : All India Reporter
A.C.J. : Accidents Claim Journal
ACT : Accidents Claim Tribunal
A.P. : Andhra Pradesh
All ER : All England Reports
AWC : Allahabad Weekly Cases
All. : Allahabad
A.L.J. : Allahabad Law Journal
A.L.T. : Andhra Law Journal
art. : article
Bom. : Bombay
Bom. L.R. : Bombay Law Reporter.
Cal. : Calcutta
C.W.N. : Calcutta Weekly Notes
C.L. Rev. : Columbia Law Review
C.B.I.B. : CBI Bulletin
C.I.C.B. : Criminal Injuries Compensation Board.
C.J.S. : Criminal Justice System
C.L.Q. : Central Law Quarterly
Cutt. L.T. : Cuttack Law Times
Cr.P.C. : Criminal Procedure Code
Cr.L.J. : Criminal Law Journal
Del. : Delhi
Ed. : Edition
Govt. : Government Law Journal
Guj. L.J. : Gujarat Law Journal
H.C. : High Court
I.J.C.C. : Indian Journal of Criminology and Criminalistic
i.e. : that is
I.P.C. : Indian Penal Code

I.P.J. : Indian Police Journal
Ibid .: In the same place (Ibidem)
I.L.R. : Indian Law Reports
J.I.H.R. : Journal of the Institute of Human Rights
J.I.L.I. : Journal of the Indian Law Institute
J.N.H.R.C.: Journal of the National Human Rights Commission
J. : Justice
JJ. : Justices
J. and K. : Jammu and Kashmir
J.T. : Judgment Today (S.C.)
Ker. : Kerala
L.Q.R. : Law Quarterly Review
L.R. : Law Reports
Ltd. : Limited
M.L.R. : Modern Law Review
M.P. : Madhya Pradesh
Mad. : Madras
Nag. : Nagpur
Ori. : Orissa
p. : Page
pp. : Pages
P and H. : Punjab and Haryana
Pat. : Patna
P.C.I.J. : Permanent Court of International Justice
Raj. : Rajasthan
S.C. : Supreme Court
S.C.C. : Supreme Court Cases
S.C.J. : Supreme Court Journal
S.C.R. : Supreme Court Report
Sec. : Section
Supra : Cited earlier
U.P. : Uttar Pradesh
U.S.S.C.R. : United States Supreme Court Report
viz. : Namely (videlicet)
v. : versus
Vol. : Volume
W.B. : West Bengal
W.L.R. : Weekly Law Report
Y.L.J. : Yale Law Journal

1

Prologue

(I) GENERAL SKETCH

Justice is the first and foremost virtue of a social institution. Justice can be ensured in any ordered society if there is an atmosphere conducive to peaceful and undisturbed existence of the society. Such an atmosphere can be provided if the state is able to ensure its basic justification and commitment of maintaining order in society and providing security to all. That was the reason why the great contractarian thinker Hobbes declared that the foremost task of legal ordering is to protect the security of life, property and contract. In the same vein the great utilitarian Jeremy Betham declared security to be the principal, indeed the paramount object of social control through law. Thus, justice and security are interrelated. Justice aims to ensure material value of security in social relations. Security relates to the control of legal norms "connected with the protection of human beings against acts of aggression, spoliation and depredation along with mitigating the effect of certain hardships, vicissitudes and hazards incident to human existence."[1] While explaining the achievement of justice as fairness John Rawls points out that each person possesses an inviolability founded on justice that even the welfare of a society cannot override. John Rawls means by it that we must never be unjust to one man in order to benefit others.[2]

In view of the requirement of security and justice as fairness the administration of justice has to take care of the benefits, rights and dignity of all segments of the society. The administration of criminal justice needs to take care of the law breaking offenders and the victims of offences committed by the offenders alike. It is common experience what Durkheim exposed in his celebrated work CRIME AS A NATURAL PHENOMENON that "a society composed of persons with angelic qualities would not be free from violation of norms of that society." It is a natural phenomenon. People differ in their values, goals and aspirations. It is not possible for all people to share sentiments to the same degree. Durkheim exposes the problem by commenting that even if it were possible "crime would not thereby disappear, it would only change its form, for the very cause which would drag up the source of criminality would immediately open up new one."[3] When the individuals violate the norms of the society and commit crime, administration of criminal justice tries to enforce rule of law, curbing its violation, maintenance of order, conviction of offender, reducing crime and rehabilitating the violators of law in society with the help of correctional institutions.

Crime has many components—offender, society and victim of crime. But victim of the crime has been a "forgotten man" in the administration of criminal justice. The entire focus of the criminal justice system has been based on the offender; to punish him or to his reformation and rehabilitation with all resources and good will available through the agencies of administration of justice—the courts and other governmental and non-governmental agencies. So long as there was no clear-cut demarcation between the criminal procedure and civil procedure, the victims of the crimes were also taken care of. As Mr. Justice V.R. Krishna Iyer (Retd.) in his Foreword to Bharat B. Das's book *Victims in Criminal Justice System* made clear, "victimology did not dawn one fine day but has been part of the code of Hammurabi (Babylon) and has been hinted at in ancient texts,

Greek, Roman and Indian." But with the emergence of clear division between the criminal procedure for criminal acts viewed as an act against the state and civil procedure dealing with civil wrongs, the right of victims of crime disappeared and lost sight of. So long as there was no clear-cut demarcation between the public law and private law, the victims had their due in administrative of justice. Though criminal law was distinguishable from most branches of private law, but was very closely related to the law of tort. Some act as test could not be used for such distinctions as the same act could be both a crime and a tort. For example, 'A' took 'B's watch, it was both tort of conversion and the crime of larceny. In Roman law *Furtum* was treated as a wrong which gave a right to compensation to the injured owner, but the thief could alternatively be punished criminally. In english common law before the enactment of the Common Informers' Act, 1951 in certain action by the common informer, the object was punishment but the penalty went to the pocket of informer. But by and by the distinction between the criminal cases and civil cases got established. Kenney defines crime as "wrongs whose sanction is punitive, and is in no way remissible by any private person, but is remissible by the Crown alone, if remissible at all." *Secondly*, crime involved liability to punishment. In such cases the prisoner suffered, but the private person wronged did not get benefit in material sense. Though in certain cases after conviction court could award restitution of stolen goods to the real owner, but the power of the Criminal Court was thought to be based merely on administrative convenience. *Thirdly*, in early age the right to punish an offender was given to the victim or his relatives. It was not approved of and state took upon itself to satisfy the blood lust and vengeance of the victim's relatives and friends by punishing the offender in a swift and brutal manner. When state took over itself to punish the offenders, by and by the victims of the crimes got neglected and overlooked. *Fourthly*, the countries adopting Anglo-Saxon adversial or accusatorial trial system instead of continental system totally denied the *locus standi* of the victim of the crime. The cumulative effect of all the above discussed developments led to development of criminology as a science of crime seeking to study the phenomenon of criminality concerning the conduct of individual behaviour prohibited by society. It dealt with causes of criminality and suggested remedies to reduce crime. It gave birth to sympathetic approach to criminal's treatment and it developed penology dealing with custody, treatment, preventions and control of crimes. This led to liberalisation in dealing with criminals and criminal justice policy put emphasis on punishment with greater opportunity for rehabilitation. The reformation through punishment got coin on philosophy that every man is born good but circumstances transform him into a criminal. The tested philosophy concerning human life may be seen in the aphorism that "if every saint has a past, every sinner has a future." The reformative approach got interwined with a rehabilative aspect to a convicted prisoner. Accused got many statutory and judicially created protections and rights. But what about poor victims of crime?

(II) VICTIM VIS-A-VIS OFFENDER

A bird's eye view of the rights of offenders in different capacities may reveal how they enjoy privileged and better position in comparison to the victims of the crimes. Under our Constitutional scheme arrested person has right to be informed of grounds of arrest, right to counsel, right to be produced before the magistrate within 24 hours of arrest, protection against self-incrimination, etc. Under Indian Penal Code such person has protection against illegal commitments and confinement; protection against causing hurt to make a statement or confession, protection against causing grievous hurt to extort confession or to compel restoration of property; protection against wrongful restraint and wrongful confinement, protection against rape, etc. Under the Code of Criminal Procedure, 1973 offender enjoys a bunch of protection, e.g. protection against arbitrary and unlawful arrest; protection against arbitrary and illegal detention in custody; right to be informed of the grounds of his arrest immediately after the arrest; right of arrested person not be subjected to unnecessary restraint; right to consult lawyer of his choice; right to be produced before Magistrate within 24 hours of arrest; protection against double jeopardy; right to be released on bail; right to get copies of the documents and statement of witness on which prosecution relies; rights of statement to police to be signed; protection against inducement and recording to confession and statements; right to insist that evidence be recorded in his presence except in some exceptional circumstances; right to have due notice of the charges; right to have an opportunity for explaining the circumstances appearing in evidence against him at the trial; right to be tried by independent, impartial and competent judge, right to submit written arguments at conclusion of the trial in addition to oral submission; right to legal aid at the expense of the state in certain cases; right to be heard about the sentence upon conviction; right to fair and speedy investigation and trial; right to appeal in cases of conviction; right not be imprisoned upon conviction in certain circumstances; right to get copy of the judgment when sentenced to imprison. Certain rights are enjoyed by the arrested person under Indian Evidence Act, 1872, for example right of voluntary confession without inducement, threat or promise, right not be put to torture for extracting confession as such confession is inadmissible; right of the accused to be presumed innocent. The Judiciary has conceded a number of fundamental rights to offenders by giving extended meaning to right to life and person liberty used under Article 21 of the Constitution of India viz. right of detenue to get a book written by him during detention to be published; right not to be put in solitary confinement; right not to be handcuffed without adequate reasons in writing; right to legal to indigent accused, right to speedy trial; right against cruel and unusual punishment, right to compensation against state excesses and atrocities or custodial death, etc.

In contrast to the offenders victims of the crime are forced to remain silent spectator. They do not have much say to see that the offender is efficiently and adequately punished by a court of law. Due to not so encouraging attitude of the criminal justice system involving police, public prosecutor and courts, the victims in a large number have been refusing to serve the criminal justice system. Even very little right of victims conceded are not very much effective. For example, the victim has a right under section 154 of the Criminal Procedure Code, 1973 to approach the police for registration of the First Information Report and in the case of refusal to register the F.I.R. to approach to the Superintendent of the police in writing and by post. Due to unwillingness of police to register the case with a view to show lesser crimes in their area or under influence of an offender belonging to a high socio-economic strata victim is discouraged and humiliated. So far as victim's approach to the Superintendent of Police is concerned, it is very well demonstrated by observation of the Himachal Pradesh High Court in *Munna Lal* v. *State of Himachal Pradesh*.[5] The Hon'ble High Court observed: "The petitioner has thereafter been knocking at one door or the other for having his F.I.R. registered. He approached the police and thereafter the Deputy Commissioner, Simla and then the Director General of Police, Himachal Pradesh but all in vain." *Secondly*, even if F.I.R. is registered and it becomes delayed, courts are likely to look at the delayed F.I.R. with alot of suspicion.[6] *Thirdly*, registration of F.I.R. also becomes unlikely in most cases where the offence is committed by the policemen themselves.[7] The victim's right to get F.I.R. registered as a last resort before the Magistrate is also discouraged in view of the highly formal and complex procedure which cannot be put in motion without the help of a legal practitioner. The victim's right to get information about the outcome of the completion of investigation is also not very much effective. Section 173(2)(ii) of the Criminal Procedure Code provides that after completion of the investigation the officer-in-charge of the police station "shall also communicate, in such manner as may be prescribed by the State Government, the action taken by him, to the person if any, by whom the information relating to the commission of the offence was first given." This provision is of not much use because it is rarely observed by the police in actual practice and if the informant is some body else other than the victim, he may not be informed at all. The right of accused to engage a private lawyer in addition to be public prosecutor under section 301(2) of the Criminal Procedure Code does not prove much effective as the lawyer such engaged will have to act under the direction of the public prosecutor and law permits such lawyer only to submit written arguments with permission of the Court and that too after the evidence is closed in the case. Though, the victim has no statutory to resist the grant of bail to the offender, however, judiciary has taken very favourable stand to the victim. In *Gram Sabha, Lakhanpur Panti* v. *Ram Deo and Another*[8] the Allahabad High Court observed: "the complainant aggrieved party may or may not have legal right of being heard but the rule of prudence and natural justice require that the aggrieved party must be afforded an opportunity to have its say personally or through a counsel of his choice, if he so desires."

(III) FACTORS NECESSITATING VICTIM-ORIENTED CRIMINAL JUSTICE JURISPRUDENCE

From progressive criminological point of view criminality appars to be a curable deviance. The Supreme Court of India very well clarified this point of view in *Mohammad Giassudin* v. *State of Andhra Pradesh*[9] when it observed, "progressive criminologists across the world will agree that the Gandhian diagnosis of offenders as patients and his conception of prison as hospitals—mental or moral—is the key to the pathology of delinquency and the therapeutic role of punishment. The whole man is a healthy man and every man is born good. Criminality is a curable deviance. Our prison should be correctional houses, not cruel iron arching the soul." But, this is the one side of the administration of criminal justice. As early as 1895 at the Prison Congress the Belgian criminologist Adolpher Pin sarcastically remarked that, "the guilty man lodged, fed, clothed, warmed, lighted, entertained, at the expense of the State in a model cell, issued from it with a sum of money lawfully earned, has paid to his debt to society; he can set his victim at defiance; but the victim has his consolation; he can think that the taxes he pays to the treasury, he has contributed towards the parental care which has guarded the criminal during his stay in prison. While the offender is being educated, housed and fed at the expense of the tax payers, the victim is left to pay for his medical expenses, perhaps to adjust to a permanent physical handicaps and to replace essential possessions that have been stolen and will never be recovered."[10]

By and by the thinking started that victims can no more be left as "forgotten people." The issue of victims suffering, reparation and rehabilitation are also the matters related to criminal justice. It got momentum with the awakened interest in victims. A new branch of study started. So long as there was no talk of victims only criminology prevailed. Thereafter victimology was conceded as extension of criminology. *The Oxford Companion To Law* described "victimology as a branch of the study of criminology, concerned with the effect on the victims of crime, physical and mental, of their experience." But this description did not present a correct picture as was explained with a view to provide corrective way to the criminal. It pointed out that "it supplies a valuable corrective sole regard for the criminal."[11] In like vein Stephen Harwitz and Karl O. Christiansen[12] argue that the concept of victimology is of recent date and its content is not always precisely described. As a sub-division of criminology, it may be defined as a study of the relation between the offenders and his victim. The discovery of the importance of the influence of alcohol in the victims of crime of violence is one example of a fruitful field of research of victimology. The traditional approach centered discussion of victimology from the angle of the criminal. Too much emphasis on the human rights of offender did not appreciate fully the seriousness of the human rights of the victims. From time to time the victim's right was also appreciated. The great utilitarian Jeremy Bentham had pleaded for victim compensation with a view to provide additional punishment and deterrence for the criminal. Raffael Garofolo pleaded for restitution as a forceful means for social defence against the law-breaker. Finally, Sara Margury Fry pleaded restitution as a reconciliation of the offender with the victim.

Victimology as a new science, separate from criminology came into existence with Benjamin Mendelson in 1937. The term was derived from the Latin "Victim" and the Greek "Logos." It means science of victims. He ceased to blame victims and started scientific dealing by extending it to include other categories of victims—apart from the victims of crime. He developed the theory of "General Victimology." It aimed at helping all kinds of victims of events beyond human control. Subsequently, he presented a theory of "extended victimology." Under this developed concept he projected to include the victims of work accidents, victims of traffic acciddents, deliquent children, the victims of Nazis, victims of genocide in general and victims of other law-breakers. 'General victimology' is built around the notion of 'victimity'. It means the 'whole of the socio-bio-psychological characteristics, common to all victims in general which society wishes to prevent and fight, no matter what determinants are."[13] Separovic (1985) proposed to deal victimology at two levels. The first level he proposed was traditional and akin to criminology. He termed it Penal Victimology dealing with victims of crime. He then proposed to deal with 'General Victimology'. It covered victims in general. For example, it deals with victims of punishable acts or accidents, victims of society, victims of State excesses, atrocities or victims of group violence. The feminist movement of 1970s and 1980s invited attention to victims of rape, domestic violence, child abuse and sexual harassment. There are certain vunerable groups. In 1968 Winslow observed, "risk of victimisation from forcible rape, robbery and burglary, are clearly concentrated on lowest income group and decreased steadily at higher income level." A more radical victimology includes victims of State—police force violence, army violence, prison system, other state violence and oppression. Now victims include both criminological and non-criminological.

(a) State's Duty to Guarantee Security and Protection

The radical or extended meaning of victimology has a human rights touch. The violation of law is not only an offence against the society but also against the person of the victim. As a member of society everybody has a right not to be victimized and if he is victimized he should have right to seek justice under the law. It is felt that it is the duty of the state to protect its members for their duty of allegiance.

President Abraham Lincoln accepted the duty of every government to give protection to its citizens irrespective of class, colour and condition.[14] In the same vein Chief Justice Waite recognized the government, duty to protect citizens. Delivering the unanimous decision of the Supreme Court of U.S.A. in *Minor* v. *Happersett*,[15] Waite C.J. made clear that allegiance and protection are reciprocal obligations. The one is compensation for the other—allegiance for protection and protection for allegiance. The Constitution of India guarantees equality to all and courts are willing to enforce security obligation of State through making the right to life and personal liberty effective under Article 21 of the Constitution.

(b) Radical International Concern

The radical meaning attached to victimology has attracted international concern. In 1979, the World Society of Victimology was formed. During 1980s many symposia were held to focus the attention on the victims of crime. In 1985 under the aegis of United Nations General Assembly Congress on Prevention of Crime and Treatment of Offender was organised wherein a Declaration on Basic Principles of Justice for Victim of Crime and Abuse of Power was made universal. It defined victims of crime in most comprehensive meaning. It adopted certain policies. Some of policies are as follows:

1. Victims should be treated with compassion and respect for their dignity. They are entitled to access to the mechanisms of justice and to prompt redress.
2. Victims should be informed of their rights in seeking redress through such mechanism. Victim must be given potential and rightful participation opportunities in proceedings instead of being just a helpless and passive spectator to those proceedings.
3. New trends in sentencing policies should be accepted so as to meet the justice to the victims of crime. Such trends should include restitution as a sentencing option; allowing agreement or adjustment between offender and victim so as to restore the losses to the victim.

The above referred U.N. Declaration of Basic Principles of Justice for Victims of Crime and Abuse of Power concerns with two parts. Part A of Declaration concerns with crime and calls on Sates to take steps to prevent victimisation and to provide victims with access to justice and fair treatment, restitution from offender and compensation from the state. In Part 'B' main emphasis is put on human rights and Declaration concerns with victims of Abuse of power. It defines victims as "persons who individually or collectively have suffered harm including physical or mental injury, emotional suffering or economic loss or substantial impairment of their fundamental rights though act of omissions do not yet constitute violations of national criminal laws but are internationally recognised norms relating to human rights. "The Economic and Social Council (ECOSOC) of the United Nations recognised the need of proper work in the field of abuse of power and to develop international means for preventing the abuse of power and redress of victims of such abuse where national channels may be insufficient.

(c) Changing Judicial Outlook

The administration of criminal justice requires reconciliation between the conflicting values. V.O. Leary and Ryane once commented on the affairs of the criminal justice system by observing, "Rarely are conflicts openly explored, and even more rarely are they handled successfully. The notion that criminal justice is a system whose parts must effectively articulate is more often employed as a pious aspiration that as something to be applied seriously."[16] However, the necessity of keeping a balance has been felt by the courts. In 1934, the great American Supreme Court Judge Mr. Justice Benjamin N. Cardozo observed in "*Synder* v. *Massachussetts*[17] that, justice, though due to accused, is due to accuser also. The concept of fairness must not be strained till it is narrowed to a filament. We are to keep balance true."[18] The disbalance in criminal justice system was felt by the great Indian Supreme Court Judge Mr. Justice V.R. Krishna Iyer. In *Rattan Singh* v. *State of Punjab*[19] exposing the apathy of law to a victim of crime, the learned judge, observed. "It is a weakness of our jurisprudence that victims of crime and the distress of the dependents of the victim do not attract the attention of law. In fact the victim reparation is till the vanishing point of our criminal law. This is the deficiency in the system, which must be rectified by the legislature."

The Judiciary is also favouring restorative Justice in the place of earlier punitive Justice. The object of traditional administration of Justice has been to punish the criminal so as deter him from criminal acts and thereby to protect the society. In this planning retributive, deterrent, preventive, denunciatory and reformative theories of punishment are applied. Now the courts have come to think of restorative justice which concerns with the restoration of victim, offender and community. It keeps into mind the healing (restoration) rather than hunting. It is primarily concerned with repairing damage done and restoring harmony. In this process the role of victim becomes very important. Restorative justice is achieved by restitution or compensation.

(d) Justice in View of Victimology—A Worldwide Phenomenon

In later half of the twentieth century there was wind of change in outlook towards the victims of crime throughout the world. United Kingdom, France, Federal Republic of Germany, Italy, Netherland, Norway, Sweden, the United States of America have provided many rights to the victims of crime. England has adopted Victim's Charter, 1996, America has adopted the Victim and Witness Protection Act, 1982, The Victims of Crime Act, 1984 and the Crime Control Act, 1990 which contain a number of principles governing the treatment of Victims of the Crimes. By the Violent Crime Control and Law Enforcement Act of 1994, The Mandatory Victims Restitution Act of 1996 and the Victim Right Clarification Act of 1997, the United States has enomously enhanced protection to the Victims of the Crime. Civil law countries like France, Germany, Italy, Sweden, Norway, Denmark and Switzerland have also conceded right to claim compensation against the state in certain cases, victim's right of participation, compensation for violence victims, etc.

(IV) STATEMENT OF PROBLEM

Social justice is the signature tune of the Indian Constitution. Preamble and Directive Principles of State Policy plan to ensure justice—social, economic and political to all. Article 14 speaks of equality before law and equal protection of laws within the territory of India. Article 21 forbids state from depriving "any person of life or personal liberty" except with the procedure established by law. Article 41 requires state to make effective provisions for "securing the right to public assistance in cases of disablement and in other cases of undeserved want. Article 51-A imposes fundamental duties on every citizen "to have compassion for living creatures", "to abjure violence" and "to develop humanism." The constitutional guarantee should include the right of the individual to remain free from being made a victim. Our constitutional commitment should have its overtone in criminal justice system.

Many countries of the world have passed comprehensive victim's code dealing with victims participation, reparation and restoration. The present study proposes to examine the Indian attempts to keep pace with victim's right in view of radical victimology. The present study plans to critically examine the sufficiency of present legislation recognising victim's right to restitution and compensation under section 357 of the Code of the Criminal Procedure. The existing criminal jurisprudence propagating and adhering the catchy Jargon that 'let the thousand guilty escape, but no innocent be punished' has played very nefarious role at least for the victims. Victims also get nothing if offenders go unidentified and unpunished. He has to remain victimized. Offences of grave intensity like communal offences, environmental offences, victims of the break down of law and order and mob violence, terrorist activities cry for redress as mass victims. Victims require fruitful justice through restorative justice and enforceable basic rights. It is to be examined in the present study whether existing criminal justice system has been able to serve the cause of victims by avoiding their neglect and due place in actual practice.

In view of the lack of higher literacy rate in India the ignorance of right may cause great disservice to the victims of crime. A mass campaign appears to be necessary to generate popular awareness about the existence of the rights of victims and thereby insuring justice to them. In India there is lack of interest in victims due to infant stage of victimology. The criminal justice system still has too much for offenders accused, prisoners and convicted persons and very little for the poor victims. A new impetus is generated through human rights awareness which appears to be conscious of the rights of victims also. Some shift is felt and by and by attempts are being made to falsify the proverb that 'Life is nothing but a competition to be criminal rather than victim'.

The victims may have rights. Their rights might have recognition but if the proper remedies are not provided, such sympathy will be bound to serve no purpose. The study makes attempt to establish the strong case of restorative justice with a view to safeguard and provide fruitful justice to victims of crimes.

New emerging challenges are more akin to aggravate the problem of victims in view new types of offences through terrorist activities. Much concern is being felt on international level. It is felt that justice is under stress on global level. At Golden Jubilee celebration of the Indian Law Institute on 24th and 25th November 2006 a international conference was held on "*Criminal Justice under stress: Transnation Perspective.* The four session were devoted to (i) Terrorism and the Criminal Justice System; (ii) Criminal Justice System—Shift from Justice Model to crime Control; (iii) International Criminal Court, and (iv) Money Laundering a menace Uncontrolled. The trend shows that victims fate will be more and badly affected and traditional thinking of restitution may not be sufficient or appreciable to do justice to the victims. A more and more insurance-based liability of state to pay compensation will be the need of hour to cope with new challenges.

(V) HYPOTHESIS AND TOOLS ADOPTED IN THE BOOK

The wind is blowing in the direction of victim—oriented criminal justice system. International law is taking lead in view of human rights movements. Other developed countries of the world are following the same track. The main focus of the book is on the issue that despite some efforts—statutory and judicial, the provisions ensuring justice to victim, and thereby inspiring their active participation in the criminal justice system, India has not achieved its intended goals and much is needed to keep Indian pace of victim-oriented justice on par with the measures adopted elsewhere in the world.

An attempt has been made to show the main trend of victim's claim, their place and rights under the criminal administration of justice in view of new concept of victimology. The Chapter 1 is devoted to the general trend towards victimology and thereby attracting victim's right and role in criminal administration of criminal justice. Chapter 2 is devoted to the role of victims in Administration of Criminal Justice in Historical Perspective and narrates how the fate of the victim's right has perceived ups and down and has ultimately shown a trend prevailing in Ancient times with many new dimensions. The study of Chapter 3 narrates march towards victim-oriented criminal justice system in view of concept of justice and its kinds, shifting paradigm from punitive justice to restorative justice along with modes of ensuring restorative justice to the victims of the crimes and assistance programes for the victims. Chapter 4 focuses a trend of the realization of victims right as a world-wide phenomenon in which United Nations is taking lead and different countries are following the norms set by the United Nations. Chapter 5 is devoted to restitutive, compensatory justice and assistance justice to the victims of crime under statutory provisions in India. In view of new victimological developments and cry for securing the victims right in as many ways as possible, the provisions securing restitutive and compensatory justice under Cr. P.C. and other statutory provisions (not technical relating criminal law field) have been discussed. The study of Chapter 6 is devoted to the activist role of Indian Judiciary in awarding compensation to the victims as a public law remedy ensuring the obligation of the state to protect the liberty and life of the people. It covers a wide range of cases of state excesses through illegal arrests and unwarranted detentions, police atrocities, custodial death and take encounters, police firing, riots and untoward happenings and compensatory justice to the victims of rape. Chapter 7 presents a critical evaluation of the whole range of study along with certain suggestions to make Indian efforts fruitful and on line with the world community.

The method adopted is more or less doctrinaire. Thus, the relevant books, articles, statutory provisions, international covenants and Declarations, judicial decisions relating to the topic have been vigorously examined and analysed. Since the study is not based on field work, the secondary sources like books and articles of the learned authors and primary sources like, judicial decisions and statutory enactment have used widely.

Notes and References

1. Bodenheimer, Edgar, Jurisprudence, Second Indian Reprint, 1997, pp. 171-72.
2. Rawls, John, A Theory of Justice (1971).
3. Durkheim, Emile, Rules of Sociological Method.
4. Kenny, Criminal Law (15th ed.) 16.
5. 1992 Cri. L.J. 1558.
6. Apren Joseph alias Current Kunju *v.* State of Kerala, A.I.R. 1973 S.C. (1973 Cri. L.J. 185): Thulika Kall *v.* State of Tamil Nadu, A.I.R. 1973 S.C. 501 and Jagannath Giri *v.* State of Bihar, 1992 Cr. L.J. 648.
7. Seraj Aslam *v.* State of U.P., 1992 Cri. L.J. 2244.
8. 1993 Cr. L.J. 3277.
9. A.I.R. 1977 S.C. 1926.
10. The Prison Congress, 1895, Summary Report (London); c.f. Schaefer, Stephen, Restitution to Victim of Crime, Stevens and Sons Ltd. London (1960), p. vii.
11. Walker, David, M., The Oxford Companion To Law, Clarendon Press: Oxford, 1980, p. 1276.
12. Hurwitz, Stephen and Christiansen, Karl O., *Criminology*, 1983, London: Geoge.
13. Thilagraj, R. and Prasanna, G., "White-Collar Crimes: A Victiomological Perspective (in) Devasia, V.V., *Human Rights and Victimology;* Dutta and Sons, Nagpur, p. 209 (211).

14. The Collected Works of Abraham Lincoln (in R. Basler (ed.), Vol. VI (1953), p. 357.
15. 88 U.S. 162 (1875).
16. Leary, V.O. and Ryane, E., *A Study of Conflict Resolution in the Criminal Justice*, National Council of Crime and Deliquency, New York (1967), p. 2.
17. 291 U.S. 97 (1934).
18. *Ibid.*, 122.
19. (1979) 4 S.C.C. 719.

2

Victim's Role in Administration of Criminal Justice in Historical Perspective

The perception of the administration of criminal justice has developed from individualistic to collectivist partnership. In the beginning the criminal justice system consisted of two parties—the offender and the offended victim. The latter started and handled the prosecution of the former. But since long scenario is changed and the place of individual has been taken up by the state. Now the two parties to criminal justice system are offender and the state and the position of the victim has been relegated to a witness. Thus, the victim's position has been relegated from earlier central position to the present prosecution's helping hand as witness.

Crime and criminal have existed throughout the history of mankind. Criminals violated the social norms and laws of the state and while doing so affected the victims. Earlier victims played vital role of Jury, Judge and executioner. Victims themselves began to spoke of the system and its shortcomings. When state through its agencies took to support and validate the version of the victims, the change came into the system. In the place of victim's vengeance and direct control state took upon itself to satisfy the victims notion of grief. In this process victim's role in criminal justice system disappeared. With the new awakening and human rights assertions again it was felt that victims should no more be neglected as "forgotten people." This feeling led to movement relating to victim's right and their role in administration of criminal justice. Thus the history of victim's role in criminal justice system is very interesting in historical perspective. It can be studied under the following heads:

(I) VICTIM'S POSITION IN ANCIENT ERA

In early times society was not well organised. Restitution to the victim of crime was ancient day practice. In absence of well organised political institution to deal with criminals by enforcing law and punishing them, the right to deal with criminals by punishing them vested with the victim himself or with the victim's near relations. They took punishment as private revenge aimed at deterrence and compensation for crime. In those days criminal victim relationship was the reflection of existence for survival and power struggle. Survival was its main basis and it was not based on the notion of responsibility. The result being that it thought that the prevention of future crime could be better achieved through ruthless retaliation and aggressively acquired compensation.[1]

With the establisation of primitive groups, the control of criminal activities became part of the social control and the offences against the individuals came to be considered as offences against the clan or tribe. and control of crime was taken by the clan or tribe leaving aside the individual. Since there was no codified law, some form of restitution and compensation was always involved in the inter-relationship between the victim and the offender. Taking over of the responsibility of social control of offences may be regarded as the emergence of the concept of collective liability.[2]

The determining factor as to seriousness of injury to the person was based on seriousness of the offence and social evaluation of the aggrieved party. Stephen Schafer referring to Ifugoa in North Luzon points out five critical factors in determination of damages:

1. The Nature of the offence;
2. The relative class and position of the litigants;
3. The solidarity and behaviour of two kinship involved in the dispute;
4. The personal tempers and reputation of the two principals (parties to dispute); and
5. The geographical position of the two kin groups.

(a) Victim's Position in Ancient India

In ancient India reparation or compensation were recognised as form of punishment. The ancient Hindu law givers fully recognised the necessity of directly compensating the victim of crime. During Sutra period awarding compensation was treated as a royal right. The Law of Manu required the offender to pay (i) compensation, (ii) expenses of cure in case of injuries to the sufferer, and (iii) satisfaction to the owner where goods were damaged. Manu says in Chapter VIII, verse 287 of the *Laws of Manu* that, "If the limb is injured, a wound (is caused) or blood (flows) the assailant shall be made to pay (to the sufferer the expenses of the cure, or the whole (both the usual amercement and expenses as a fine to the kind."[3] Again in chapter VIII, verse 288, Manu said, "He who damages the goods of another, be it intentionally or unintentionally, shall give satisfaction to the (owner) and pay to the kind a fine equal to damage."[4] Thus Manu provided for two types of payment by offender—one by way of direct reparation to the victim of crime and other to the king by way of fine. Similar, view was expressed by Brihaspati when be observed, "He who injures a limb or divides it, or cuts it off, shall be compelled to pay the expresses of curing it; and (who forcibly took an article in a quarrel restore) his plunder."[5] Brihaspati has also spoken for punishment for selling sub standards or blemish articles. He said: "A merchant who conceals the blemishes of an article which he is selling or mixes bad and good articles together, or sells (old articles) after repairing them shall be compelled to give a double quantity (to the purchaser) and to pay fine equal (in amount) to the value of the article."[6]

Similarly, the Law of Vishnu and Yajnavalkya also provided for compensation to the victims of crime for their injury. In the case of fraudulent or defective articles Yajnavalkya, Nanid and Brihaspati fixed twice of amount to purchaser to be given and also a fine of an equal amount.[7]

Katyayan gave a detailed scheme of restitution for different categories of restitution for different categories of theft. He made persons responsible for maintaining order and providing security to persons. Thus,

1. If property was stolen from houses in a village, the thief catchers had to pay to the owners;
2. If thief was not found king had to make the guarding officers and wardens of the country to pay the price of stolen property;
3. In the case of property stolen in the village, the head man of the village was asked to restore by paying value of the stolen property.
4. In the case of the property being stolen in a forest, the king had to restore the stolen property or its price.[8]

The primary duty of restitution was fixed on the King. The King's liability of restitution if completed could be recovered form the thief. Thus, whatever was stolen from any person in one's kingdom was to be restored by the king. He had to search for the thing lost and if found (after he paid the price to the owner) the king could retain the article himself. In the case the thief was caught and article stolen was not recovered from him, the king was to restore the thing himself or he was to make the thief pay according to King's pleasure.[9]

As to the initiation of proceeding victim or his kin's had to play active role. Manu said that the King or his officers should not start any litigation. There could be no litigation unless the person injured complained before the king.9 This rule was more or less rigidly followed is narrated by the trial scene in *Mrichchhakatika*. In Mrichchhakatika although the King's brother-in-law Sakara had laid a complaint before the court that Charudutta had killed Vasantsena. The court did not allow it as Sakara had no right in the matter. The Judge sent massage for Vasantsena's mother whether she had any complaint.[10] But in the course of time exceptions had to be recognised and in certain cases prosecution could be started by king or his officers.

In Ramayan written by great seer Valmiki, there is a story of a dog beaten up by a Brahmin. A dog was beaten up by a Brahmin who thought himself to be unpurified by the shadow of the dog. The dog went to the court of Lord Rama as a complainant-victim. The dog presented his case before Lord Rama narrating his innocence and the unwarranted provocation of the Brahmin beating him. Lord Rama patiently heard the case of the dog, paid due attention. But due to lack of precedent on the point did not come to definite conclusion as to the punishment. Lord Rama asked the dog itself how the wrong doer could be punished to meet the end of Justice. The dog suggested Lord Rama to make the wrong doer Brahamin Kaulpati (Mathadheesh) of Kalanjar Math. To the great surprise of Lord Rama and his courtiers the dog narrated odds and disadvantages of the office of a Mathadheesh. According to him the Brahmin could be punished in that way. The story narrates the victim's participation in administration of justice.[11]

(b) Victim's Role in Babylon and Other Countries

The law of Moses also provided for compensation to the affected persons by giving four-fold restitution for stolen sheep and five-fold for the more useful one.[12] Babylon presents the earliest code popularly known as Code of Hammurabi (C. 1728–1686 B.C.). The king of ancient Babylon codified the law in which there are provisions for generously compensating the victims. The restitution was certain in cases of stolen property be it recovered or not. The amount of restitution also varied. Thus, (1) the theft of goods while they were being transported was punishable by a five-fold restitution; (2) the embezzlement of a merchant money by one of his employees required a three-fold payment. Even in case of undetected thief victim was restituted by the state. The condition in such cases was that the victim had to itemized his property in the presence of God.[13] Some examples are presented below from the Code of Hammurabi:

Section 22: If a man has committed robbery and is caught, that man shall be put to death.

Section 23: If a robber is not caught, the man so robbed shall formally declare whatever he had lost before a God and the city mayor on whose territory or district the robbery has been committed shall replace whatever he has lost for him.

Section 24: If (it is) the life (of the owner that is lost) the city or the mayor shall pay one manch of silver to his kins folk.

The code provided for different punishment and every victim was averaged and compensated according to his status. Restitution and vengeance were the main theme of punishment in ancient period. The Hommurabi Code had enormous impact on Palestinian law and there is much similarity and Hommurabi Code and the restitution to be found in Old Testament. Victim of property stolen was compensated by four to five times of the property stolen. Germanic tribes were more right than those of the Romans. In the time of Alford and his Dooms (Dooms of Alford) the blood feud was invoked only after the failure of the victim's request for compensation. The priority was given to monetary compensation on request of the victim. In German tribes too the victim's status, age, sex as well as the nature of crime were the deciding factors for restitution. Under Roman Twelve Tables written by ten commissioners in 451 B.C. a thief was to pay double of the stolen property but the amount increased if the property stolen was found during the resisted execution of the house search. Blood-feud faded out in the course of time and physical retribution began to be replaced by financial compensation. Compensation was negotiated between the kins of the victims and offenders.

(II) VICTIM'S ROLE IN MEDIEVAL PERIOD

With the stability of community and tribes settling down reaction to injury of loss became less severe. With a view to minimise the trouble of perpetual vendetta[14] compensation to the victim served to mitigate to blood feuds. Indeed the medieval era came as the golden age of the victims. Criminal justice served victim's private or personal interest. The victim of the crime occupied most advantageous position in criminal administration. The settlement for injuries became a private compromise. There were certain advantages in compromise through compensation. *Firstly,* it was thought necessary to provide compensation for offences against persons in order to prevent the socially disintegrating effects of blood feud.[15] *Secondly,* compensation served two purposes—the purpose of humiliating criminal to some extent by giving compensation and satisfying the victim's desire of revenge.[16] *Thirdly,* it was felt that even homicide could be atoned by a certain fine of cattle and sheep and family of the victim got satisfied to the advantage of the public weal. If avoided quarrels which were most dangerous to a free state.[17]

In medieval era compensation and restitution was closely related to punishment and was temporarily included in penal law. However, the penal law of communities during that period was not law of crime but a law of torts.[18] Thus, composition combined punishment with damages was applied only to private wrongs and not to public crimes. The relationship between the criminal and victim was viewed only in terms of victim's revenge emotion and its satisfaction by accepting compensation. After acceptance of compensation by the injured party, that party was fully avenged the criminal procedure was complete. The payment of compensation was made entirely to the victim or his family. The amount of compensation depended and varied according to nature and extend of injury, age, rank, sex, and prestige of the victim. Thus, a "free-norm man is worth more than a slave, a grown up more than a child, a man more than a woman and person of rank more than a freeman."

(III) DECLINE IN POSITION OF VICTIM

(a) End of Golden Age of the Victim and Emergence of the Concept of Double Payment

The golden age of victim domination began to decline with the emergence of community power exceeding over the power of the individual. Community began to play vital role in bringing about reconciliation between the criminal and the victim. It resulted in claiming of King's share in compensatory amount. The compensation paid by offender was divided into two parts. Part of compensation was paid to the victim and another part went to the King. In Germanic fine was spitted between victim known as *Wergild* and the community (ruler) known as—*Fried ensgeld*. The Anglo-Saxon followed the same pattern and compensation for criminal offences consisted of two types of payments. One type of compensation was given to the victim and his family (*Wer* for homicide, *bot* for the other injuries) and other type of compensation was given to ruler/King (*Wite*).

This development further strengthened the claim of King or state and it began to claim all monetary compensation due to a victim. It was done in the name of crime as a 'breach of King's peace'. Thus, State monopolized the institution of punishment and the rights of the injured were slowly separated from the penal law. Composition as the obligation to pay damages became separated from criminal law and became a special field of civil law. As a consequence, the victim was stipped-off financial compensation and psychological satisfaction of avenging crime. With this development the 'golden-age' of the victim came to an end.[19]

(b) Decline of Victim's Role in Criminal Justice

In post-Middle era a centralised legal system developed. The role of State became most prominent in criminal justice. The concept of victim's right of restitution and compensation gradually disappeared from criminal law field and instead became incorporated in to civil law. Victim's role in criminal law was ignored and victim became the "poor relation" of the criminal law. Crime was taken as an act against the State.[20] This led State to assume the role of the prosecutor and monopolized the institution of punishment.

This happened so as the personalised system of administration was changed in impersonal state-run-system. In this process victim was virtually forgotten. The interest of the State overshadowed and supplanted the interest of the victim. The result was that there remained no connection between restitution and punishment and the two got severed. A clear separation of the area of compensation and restitution came into existence. It was known as civil law quite separate from the criminal law. This new development resulted into: (i) decline of penological importance of restitution, and (ii) non-recognition of victim's personal role in crime. It became subject of civil liability and victim could claim his right to be compensated for loss was to seek help of the civil justice system.[21]

(IV) VICTIM'S ROLE IN MODERN PERSPECTIVE: RESURRECTION

The historical account shows that the original rationale for restitution disappeared over the years, but its potential itself never completely disappeared as a criminal sanction. After the eclipe of centuries it has resurrected. Throughout the world and on international plane it has attracted the legal historian and comparative lawyers. It needs serious study: why, for instance, have schemes to compensate innocent victims of crime flourished in present decades of twentieth century after failing to flower in earlier periods of criminal law reforms.[22]

Much of the ignoring of victim's right was found due to the concept of State as police state or *laissez-faire* showing indifference with the cause of victims restitution and other welfare programmes. With the change of the concept of state from *laissez-faire* to welfare state restitution and compensation came to be recognised. By and by writers having public concern or legal and political thinkers began to recognise the victim's problems. In famous work *Utopia* Sir Thomas More advocated in 1516 that (i) offender should be required to provide restitution to the victim, and (ii) offender should be required to labour at public works.[23] The suggestion of putting offender to public work and providing restitution to the victim from its income was also suggested by the great philosopher Herbert Spencer. In 1847 Bonneville de Marsangy outlined the plan for reparation of victims and argued later at many places. At the International Prison Congress held in Stockholm in 1878 many participants proposed to return to old scheme of reparation to the injured.[24] Reparation was suggested as "a matter of justice and social security" by

Raffaele Garofalo at International Prison Congress held in Rome in 1885.[25] Again in 1890 at the International Prison Congress held at St. Petesberg and in 1891 at the International Penal Association Congress held at Christiana, the problem of reparation to victim was discussed at length. The following conclusions were drawn:

1. Modern law does not sufficiently consider the reparation due to injured parties;
2. In the case of petty offence, time should be given for indemnification; and
3. Prisoner's earning in prison might be utilized for this end.

During discussions in subsequent International Prison Congress held in Paris in 1895 the harshness of law was exposed in relation to victims *vis-a-vis* the offender. It was widely pleaded that offender should make reparation to victim. This aspect could be taken into consideration while allowing suspension of sentence or conditional release after imprisonment.[26] The philosophy of administration of criminal justice pleaded was that 'the deliquent be punished and the injured party reimbursed'. However, the Brussel Sixth International Penitentiary Congress of 1900 could not arrive at any definite proposal as to providing restitution to the victim or utilising prisioner's earning in prison as compensation to the victim.

The problem of restitution of the victims has also attracted the attention of great penologists. Penologist take a balanced and compromising stand by adopting a process of self-determinate sentence as a means of compensating victims of crime and rehabilitating offenders. During the later half of twentieth century a strong plea gathered momentum that sentence is to be determined according to the willingness and co-operation of the offender to pay restitution to his victim. If the offender chooses to restitute victim out of his private money or earning in jail, the sentence may be reduced. The victim of crime is to be compensated for physical and psychological damage sustained. The courts at discretion may also levy supplementary fines.

The study in the coming chapter will further show the increasing role of victim or at least plea for giving more and more chances of active participation of victims in the criminal justice system.

Notes and References

1. Das, Bharat B., *Victims in the Criminal Justice System*, APH Publishing Corporation, New Delhi (1997).
2. Schafer, Stephen, Victimology: *The Victim and His Criminal*, Reston, Virginia (1977) p. 11.
3. *The Laws of Manu* (in) *Secred Book of East* by Max Muller, Vol. 25, Oxford University Press, Oxford (1986). p. 304.
4. *Ibid.*, p. 305.
5. Brihaspati (in) Max Muller, *Secred Books of East*, Vol. 33, Chapter XXII, verse 10, Oxford University Press, Oxford (1886), p. 360.
6. *Ibid.*
7. Law of Vishnu, verses 75, 76, Law of Yajnavalkya 11, 226. 10, Narada N. 118.
8. Kane, P.V. (e.d.), *Text of Katyayana*, p. 98, quoted from N.C. Sen Gupta, *Evolution of Ancient Indian Law*, Eastern Law House, Calcutta, 1953 p. 304.
9 Manu, VIII 43.
10. Sen, Gupta, N.C., *The Evolution of Ancient Indian Law*, Eastern Law House, Calcutta, 1953, p. 56.
11. Valmiki, *Ramayanam—Uttar Kandam: Prakshit Sarga*—1 and 2.
12. Fry, Margrey, *Arms of the Law* (London), 1951, p. 124.
13. Barke, J.L., *We are All Victims*, Peel Press, London, (1978), p. 171.
14. Barnes, H.E. and Teeters, N.K., *New Horizons of Criminology*, Prentice Hall, Englewood Cliff. N.J. (1944), pp. 400-01).
15. Tyler noted such effect in Arbia, Tyler, E.B. *Anthropology* New York.
16. Henting, Hans Von, *Punishment, its Origin, Purposes and Psychology*, London, 1937, p. 215.
17. Tacitus noted such effect of compensation to victim in relation to ancient Germans cited from Das, Bharat B., *Victim in Criminal Justice System* (1997), p. 42.
18. Cohen, E. Irving, 'The Integration of Restitution in Probation Services (in) *Journal of Criminal Law and Criminology*, Vol. 34 (1994), p. 315.
19. Emerton, Ephrasim, *Introduction to the History of the Middle Age*, Boston (1888), p. 87.
20. Das, Bharat B., *Victim in the Criminal Justice System* (1997), p. 45.
21. *Ibid.*, p. 46.
22. Chappel, Duncan, "Emergence of Austratin Schemes to Compensate Victims of Crime", *Southern California Law Review*, Vol. 43, p. 69.

23. More, Sir Thomas, *Utopia* (J.C. Collin ed. 1904), pp. 23-24 Sir Thomas More's views are comparable to Bruce R. Jacob, "Reparation or Restitution by the Criminal Offender to his Victim; Applicability of an Ancient Concept in the Modern Correctional Process", *Journal of Criminal Law, Criminology and Political Science*, Vol. 61 (1976), 162.
24. Sutherland, Erwin H. and Cressey, Donalf R., *Principles of Criminology*, J.B. Lipponocot, Philadephia (1966), p. 331.
25. Garofalo, Raffaele, *Criminology*, Boston (1914), pp. 434-35.
26. Barrows, Report on the Sixth International Prison Congress, Brussel (1900), pp. 25-26.

3

March Towards Victim-oriented Criminal Justice System

There is feeling in some quarter that when there was no developed system of criminal administration of justice the victim or the actual sufferer of the crime was better protected. Thus, Barnes and Teeters in the their celebrated work *New Horizons in Criminology* commented that "our barbarian ancestors were wiser and more just than we are today for they adopted the theory of restitution to the injured, whereas we have abandoned this practice to the determined of all concerned."[1]

The world is moving faster than the law establishing a legal system. Law must be stable but it cannot remain stand still. According to the societal needs and developments law has to keep pace with challenges posed by newly created situations. It has to safeguard the interests of members of the society, keep balance between their conflicting interests and provide security to all. Law achieves the required purposes through effective administration of Law ensuring behaviours of the people according to the legally prescribed norms. Criminal law represents the collective definition of those behaviour to which every individual has to conform and to punish for it violation. Criminal law is one of the linking pins that hold various components of criminal justice together as a system.

Justice being the highest goal of a system is administered by the courts in accordance with law. Justice is bond which holds society together. Justice is not a static concept. It has protean vitality according to the needs of the society. It attempts to hold society together by ensuring faith in objectivity, lawfulness, fairness and beneficiency to all.

The study in the foregoing chapter revealed how the victims of crime experienced inconvenience, neglect and humiliation by depriving them their role in administration of criminal justice. After a long eclipse of middle ages some rays of hope were seen with the change of the concept of the state from *laissez-faire* to social service or welfare State. Accordingly the victim's fate in administration of criminal justice got sympathetic considerations.

An attempt will be made in this chapter to analyse the concept of justice evolved and developed by the courts through judicial pronouncements and by legal luminaries and criminal law thinkers. The study will show how the static or status-oriented juridical .concept of justice has given way to corrective and restorative justice.

(I) THE CONCEPT OF JUSTICE AND ITS KINDS

Justice is goal which is to be achieved. It has protean face. It aims to solve the problem of "good society." But it has been explained by thinkers according to their own vision of the social problems faced at their times. Thus, Plato viewed justice as having the element of harmonious relation between various parts of the social organism. Plato came to justify division of role to different classes—rulers, auxiliaries and producing class like farmers, artisans or traders. All classes were expected to play their role keeping in view the organic unity of the collective whole.[2] Aristotle viewed justice from different angle. To him justice consists in "some sort of equality." He advocated for 'distributive justice' but also wished to smoothen it by corrective justice. The corrective justice had due regard for victim which shall be discussed a little ahead. Aristotle's concept of justice as 'some sort of equality,[3] was also not free from blemish. It tolerated the institution of slavery and dominion of the male over female. Some jurists have advocated for equalisational justice. Pointing out the egalitarian view of justice the American sociologist Lester Ward said that justice consists in the "enforcement of society of an artificial equality in social conditions which are naturally unequal."[4] With a view to fulfiling all the individual needs Karl Marx and Fredrick Engels thought justice as process of equalization of resources and economic status. Spencer gave more weightage to freedom than equality. For him, "Everyman is free to do that which he will, provided he infringes not the equal freedom of any other man."[5] John Rawl's conception of justice is composed of two cardinal principles: (1) Each person is to have an equal right to the most extensive basic liberty compatible with a similar liberty for others; and (2) social and economic inequalities are to be arranged so that they can reasonably be expected to be to every one's advantage, and in such a manner that the positions and offices to which they attach are open to all.

In field of criminal law and administration of criminal justice it is acceptable that social ordering is based on realization that people desire to live together rather than die from violence. People react adversely against action of others causing them bodily or mental suffering. The person who does so is offender and needs to be punished. He also inflicts harm on other person known as victim of his criminal act and such person also needs justice to be done to him.

For the purposes of giving a clear picture of the justice from the point of view of the 'penal couple', i.e. offender and the victim, justice may be divided into—

(i) Distributive Justice and Corrective Justice, and
(ii) Civil and Criminal Justice.

(i) Distributive and Corrective Justice

Artistotle divided justice into 'distributive' and 'corrective'. Distributive justice primarily concerned with the allocation of rights, powers, duties or burdens to the members of a society or group. It requires equal distribution among equals. Treating like cases alike and to meet out fair and equal treatment to all was the primary objective of distributive justice. He regarded justice as meaning either what is lawful or what is fair and equal. Thus, distributive justice aims at securing a balance or equilibrium among the members of society by distribution of honour and wealth among the citizens and works according to ratio of merit of the particular society. By equal distribution based on merit he meant that equal things should be given to equal persons and unequal things to unequal persons. The standard for equality was to be measured by that of the merit and civic excellence. Thus, if 'X' is twice as deserving as 'Y', his (share) should be twice as large.[6]

The purpose of maintaining equilibrium in society by distributive justice may not be served always and it may be upset. Such a situation may be handled by corrective justice. Aristotle distinguished corrective justice from distributive justice. To illustrate it if a member of the community has encroached upon the rights, privileges or property of another person, corrective justice will return to the victim and which belonged to him or compensate him for his loss. Thus, corrective justice is consequential. It comes into play when the norms of distributive justice have been violated by a member of a community. In such a situation it becomes necessary to make amends for a wrong or deprive a party of an unjustified gain.[7] The corrective justice is also known as remedial justice. Corrective justice is administered by a court or other organ of the state invested with judicial or quasi-judicial authority. The chief fields of corrective justice may be contracts, torts and crimes. The disequilibrium caused is the field of contract may be balanced by way of awarding damages. In cases of torts award of compensation will be the proper remedy. In the field of criminal law disequilibrium is so caused as to affect the society in general and the victim in the particular. It is balanced in the case of former by imposing sentence upon the convicted offender. In latter case it is corrected by providing restitution or compensation to the victims of crime. Thus, corrective justice acts to restore *status quo*.

(ii) Civil and Criminal Justice

Administration of justice involves certain procedure for enforcement rights. Nature of rights, procedure for enforcement and remedy provided divide justice into civil and criminal. Criminal justice involves enforcement of criminal law. As administration of justice is outcome of the enforcement of rights and obligation of individuals and to punish a wrong-doer, the courts adopt certain methods and procedure to achieve the end of justice. 'Administration of justice' involves the maintenance of rights and duties within a politically organised community by means of the physical force of the State. There are three main components of administration of justice: the State, the law and securing obedience to law by means of the physical force of the state. The nature of law involved, the remedy sought and State agencies involved may be termed as administering civil justice or criminal justice.

Civil justice is administered by enforcement of private rights whereas criminal justice is administered by enforcement of public rights. The former involves civil wrong and the latter criminal wrong. Blackstone divided wrongs into two species—private wrongs and public wrongs. Civil wrongs are an infringement or privation of the private or civil rights belonging to individuals. The commission of civil wrongs results into civil injuries. On the other hand criminal wrongs or public wrongs involve breach and violation of public rights and duties which affect the whole community considered as a community. They are distinguished by harsher appellation of crimes and misdemeanors.

Civil and criminal wrongs are distinguishable according to their nature of affective individual and the state. However, the distinction between the two may not be always very clear. Some wrongs to the state involve public nature, but by law they are treated as civil wrongs. For example, a refusal to pay taxes is offence against the state and involves suit by the state but for the sake of enforcement it is like a civil wrong recoverable in the same manner in which money lent by a private individual is recovered. Likewise breach of a contract made with the State is not a criminal offence. There are a number of examples wherein State is necessarily involved and is injured party but the wrongs committed to State are civil wrong, e.g. action for recovery of debts, action for recovery of damages, or for restoration of public property or for the enforcement of a public trust. On the other hand, some civil wrong are of more serious nature and may involve a civil injury or a crime. The negligence of a contractor may cause greater harm to society and may involve action of criminal nature too. However, some workable distinction is maintained between the civil justice and criminal justice.

Civil justice is administered by one set of courts known as civil courts. They adopt civil procedure, i.e. filing suit of claim by the plaintiff against the defendant. The successful civil proceeding may result into a judgment for damages or in a judgment for the payment of a debt, or restitution or decree for specific performance, or in an order of the delivery of possession of land or in a decree of divorce and other alike reliefs.

The object of civil justice through enforcing or maintaining the rights by civil proceedings involves enforcement of two type of rights; firstly, primary rights and secondly, sanctioning or remedial rights. Primary rights are involved when primary obligation is not fulfilled. Such rights are also known as antecedent or sanctioned or enjoyment rights. Secondary rights are known as restitutory, sanctioning or remedial rights. Primary rights exist on their own and are not dependent commission of wrong. The examples of primary rights are the right of reputation, the right in respect of one's own person, etc. The secondary or remedial rights are involved where the primary right is infringed. They result as consequence of the violation of primary rights. By enforcing secondary rights the courts provide remedies.

Criminal justice is administered in a different set of courts known as criminal courts. The criminal proceeding is started by the State. If a criminal proceeding succeeds the result as a general trend will be the punishment of the wrongdoer. The basic object of criminal justice is to punish the wrongdoer. Punishments may range from capital punishment to fine or in a binding over to keep the peace, release upon the probation, etc.

Since crimes are more harmful in their consequences than civil wrongs, criminal justice has to take care of the society and that is reason why its main purpose is to punish the person committing the crime. State takes to punish the wrongdoer for security of the society. The most important question then arises what is purpose of punishment? Does it aim at achieving certain ends of criminal justice or it is in itself an end of the administration of criminal justice?

From the time immemorial a number of theories of punishment have been advocated. Broadly speaking, they may be divided into two categories. The oldest, primitive and nearer to human instinct view is that purpose of the punishment is retribution. The offender must be made to suffer for his criminal act. The other view is that the end of criminal justice is to protect and add to the welfare of the State and society along with ensuring protection and justice to the common people. Now retributive purpose of punishment has waned into a relic of primitivity because civilized society has realised that retribution cannot solve the problem of escalating criminal offences. The emphasis has been transposed from retribution to cure and reform so as the original man can be recreated from the ailing criminal.[8]

The above revolutionary change in the outlook of criminologists is further supported by emergence of human face of criminal justice. To quote the Hon'ble Supreme Court of India in *Mohd. Giasuddin* v. *State of U.P.*[9]: "It is a truism, often forgotten in the hidden vendetta in human bosoms that barbarity breeds barbarity and injury recoils as injury, so that if healing the mentally or morally maimed or malformed man (found guilty) is the goal, awakening the inner being, more than torturing through exterior compulsions holds out better curative hopes."[10]

With the emergence of human rights jurisprudence the criminal justice system has got transformed with new dimension softening the rigour of earlier motivation of punishment.

The criminal justice system now aims to ensure the following:

1. The process of criminal administration be humanised.
2. Equality in all respects should be ensured and all sorts of arbitrariness be controlled.
3. Liberty, security and dignity be assured to all.
4. A person coming to prison must enjoy human dignity. He does not become a non-person.
5. Human rights are basic element of correctional justice on Gandhian philosophy hate the crime, but not the criminal.
6. Prison should not be considered as a 'house of captives' dominated by punitive approach, rather it should be perceived as a "correctional institution."
7. Criminal justice system should motivate public participation in process of prevention of crime.
8. The system should facilitate on over all growth of human personality without fear.
9. Rule of Law has to be enforced on the basis equity, fairness and due process.

Criminal justice system aims at ensuring prevention of crime and enforcement of law or behalf of the citizens. The object of criminal justice system is to ensure social harmony and co-operation. It views to provide and ensure justice to all the segments of society. The aim of criminal justice is not limited to ensure justice to society against the criminal. It also makes effort to ensure justice to criminals also.

The need of hour is to keep and maintain a proper balance in the scales of criminal justice. In view of the adoption of our accusatorial or adversary system of criminal justice the poor victims of crime have been entirely overlooked in view of the misplaced too much sympathy for the criminal. Now a healthy trend is developing and a talk of *Crimino-Victim* justice is cropping up in view of the development of a criminal law jurisprudence termed as victimology. In 1958-59 Dr. Stephen Schafer of the University of Maryland had conducted a study. He put a number questions aiming at recognising the rights of the victims. Some of the important questions were as follows:

1. Whether the victim or his dependent has any legal right to claim restitution or damages from the offender;
2. If so, to what offences his rights applies;
3. Whether damages are restricted to compensation for financial loss only or any other non-material injury;
4. What should be the manner of recovery and how restitution works in practice; and
5. What should be the nature of jurisdiction.

One the idea or plea of taking into the consideration of the "forgotten man" began to have taken place a shift was discernible from traditional theories of punishment to the emerging concept of restorative justice.

(II) CRIMINAL JUSTICE SYSTEM: SHIFTING PARADIGM FROM PUNITIVE JUSTICE TO RESTORATIVE JUSTICE

As it is common understanding that by punishing a criminal justice is done to society. It fulfils the demand of society through cry for justice. But justice remains only two dimensional as recognising involvement and effect on criminal and the society. In this process the third dimension gets overlooked. To do justice with the victim who bears the burnt of the crime and check the plight of the wailing victim, it is necessary for the criminal justice to give receptive ear to their cause. With this end a new concept of "restorative justice" has to be added as an additional aspect of criminal justice.

The study of the concept of justice from different angles will show the development of such a trend favourable to the victim.

(A) Basic Postulates of Punitive Justice

Punitive justice serves the purpose of punishing the offender in accordance with law. Purpose of punishment can be one or more of the following :

1. Deterrent

To deter people from committing crime. Punishment serves as a lesson to the others who feel that if they commit crime they will not be spared. It is thought that the commission of every offence should be made "a bad bargain for the offender."

2. Preventive

Aiming to prevent a repetition of the offence. It concentrates on the prisoner but seeks to prevent him from committing offence again in future. The offender is made incapable of repeating the offence.

3. Retributive

It aimed at treating offender in like manner in which he had treated other person. Person wronged was allowed to take revenge from the wrongdoer. The principle of "an eye for an eye", "a tooth for a tooth" was recognized and followed. It is grounded in vengeance. At present it rests on principle that sentence must be in proportion to crime.

4. Denunciatory

It emphatically aims at denunciation of crime through severe punishment.

5. Reformative

It aims to reform the criminal and the claimation of the criminal to useful citizenship. It treats criminal as a mentally sick person who needs clinical treatment.

No single theory is sufficient. Nor it is acceptable for all the time. Though reformation is regarded as the dominant objective of a punishment and during incarceration, every effort should be made to recreate good man out of a convicted prisoner but it cannot be pressed too far. The principle of proportionality has to be accepted as a standard norm of awarding punishment. It should neither be too hard nor too soft. The principle behind awarding punishment was very well explained by Jeremy Bentham:

"The principal object of punishment, however, is the

> prevention from crime and the measure of punishment must, consequently, vary from time to time according to the prevalence of a particular form of crime and other circumstances. An amount of severity may be very appropriate at one time which would be quite uncalled for at another. It may generally be taken as a same principle to follow, that punishment should be made as moderate as is consistent with the object aimed at punishment in excess is opt to defeat its own object, and to produce a reaction of popular feeling, as experience shows. To shut a man up in prison longer than is really necessary is not only bad for the man himself, but also it is a useless piece of cruelty and economically wasteful and a source of loss to the community."[11]

Criminal law adheres in general to the principle of proportionality in prescribing liability according to the culpability of each kind of criminal conduct. Just deserts should be the basis of punishment. Too much sympathy shown to the criminal may become unproductive and may result into some very undesirable practical consequences. Commenting upon the leniency shown to the criminals Mr. Justice Arijit Pasayat observed in *State of U.P.* v. *Virendra Prasad*[12] in the following words:

> "The practice of punishing all serious crimes with equal severity is now unknown in civilized societies, but such a radical departure from the principle of proportionality has disappeared from the law only in recent times on account of misplaced sympathies to the perpetrator of the crime leaving the victim or his family is oblivion."[13]

In the above situation of proportionality principle courts look at doing justice to the society and the victim on the one hand and to the offender on the other. The above referred case and in some other cases,[14] the Supreme Court of India has taken note of victim's point of view. But the real purpose of victim's right protection is not served because the object of punishment is to protect the society and to deter the criminal. To quote justice Arijit Pasayat, "it is expected that the court would operate the sentencing system so as to impose such sentence which reflects the conscience of the society and the sentencing process has to be stern where it should be."[15]

Different theories explaining the purpose of punishment under a criminal justice system do not pay much heed to the neglected part of the by-product of crime-victim. He still remains a "forgotten man" under the criminal justice system. By awarding severe punishment to a criminal no material justice can be done to the victim of the crime. S.V. Joga Rao rightly exposes the problem faced by victim. He points out that the injured party is not always adequately served at civil courts and in criminal law he often takes a back seat. Having given his evidence, he stands aside and watches the offended majesty of public justice being satisfied by conviction and sentence. He himself is fortunate if he gets compensation or even his expenses. Often he must have recourse to the civil courts to reclaim his property, and not infrequently, may have suffered a loss or injury for which he can't be recompensed."[16]

(B) Restorative Justice

To do justice to the victim requires innovative idea of restorative justice. It shows a paradigm change in sentencing policy which allows or prefers to listen to the wailing of the victims. It emphasizes the need to took into the matters a fresh. Rehabilitation of the prisoner need not be by closing eyes towards the suffering victims of the offence. Restorative justice is a collective term for variety of theories concerned with restoration of victim, offender and community. Many other terms have been used as synonyms of restorative justice so as to given broader perspective of justice. Thus, such terms include positive justice, community justice, re-integrative justice, relational justice and transformative justice. The[17] main emphasis of restorative justice is about healing rather than hurting. The proponents of restorative justice view problem of criminal justice system from the angle of all the components. An integrative approach to crime, conflict and justice is becoming demand of new development. Howard Zehrvery nicely indicated this shift in paradigm of justice in the following words:

> "We define crime as an offence against the state. We define justice as the establishment of blame and the imposition of pain under the guidance of right rules. I think it essential to remember that this definition of crime and justice, as common sensical as it may seem, is only one paradigm, only one possible way of looking at crime and at justice. We have been so dominatd by our assumption that we often assume it is the only way, to approach the issue. It is not, it is not the only possible model or paradigm of justice—not logically and historically."

The quest of Howard Zehrvery for evolving new paradigm of justice with restorative vision is a welcome move. It has to take into account whole range of social and impersonal conflict. There are two approaches as to the plea of restorative or reparative theories. As a matter of fact restorative justice does not represent a particular theory of punishment. It is a way of argument suggesting that sentence should move away from punishment of the offender towards restitution and reparation, aimed at restoring the harm done and calculated accordingly. *Firstly,* it is victim-oriented and *secondly,* it encompasses the notion of reparation to the community for the effects of crime. As Professor Ashworth of Oxford University Centre for Criminological Research points out, restorative and reparative theories "envisage less resort to custody, with enormous community-based sanctions requiring offenders to work in order to compensate victims and also contemplating support and counselling for offenders to reintegrate them into the community."[18] Such theories have two aspects. *Firstly,* they tend to act on a behavioural premise similar to rehabilitation, and *secondly,* their political premise is that compensation for victim should be rcognised as more important than notions of just punishment on behalf of the State.

The victim-oriented measure adopted by legal systems

based on restorative rationale providing for compensation into the sentencing system appear to fulfil the proper balance between the different interest groups. To quote Garland, "institutions are the scenes of particular conflicts as well as being means to a variety of ends so it is no surprise to find that each particular institution combines as a number of often incompatible objectives, and organizes the relations of often antagonistic interest group."[19]

Restorative justice serves the purpose of repairing damage done and restoring harmony. The role of victim is very important in this respect. Restorative justice envisages two dimensions of viewing the problem from the angle of process and value assessment. As Braithwaite points out as a process it involves all persons relating to harm—the offender, victim and society and as value assessment it encourages significance of re-integration and respect.[20]

The idea of restorative justice goes still further. It proposes not to involve only victims and offenders but also the community. It has the following value preferences. *First,* from the angle of victim it encourages forgiveness to be preferred over punishment and retribution and thereby to achieve reintegration. Victim and his kinsmen or representative need to be given active role in resolution of the conflict arising out of crime. From the point of view of offender it also requires active part to be played by the offender realising his responsibility for wrong done to the victim. Offender should be ready to seek apology from the victim for wrong done to him and should also be willing to pay him compensation as a means of reparation. Thus, the restorative justice envisages that the old way of thinking about crime must give way no new priorities. Once the facts of crime is established the priority should not be the punishment inflicted to the offender with a view to satisfy the notion of retributional justice of victim or the society. The priority should be to meet the victim's needs as to provide him relief from further victimisation or continuance of the earlier one. The other priority should be to enable the offender to be fully aware of the damage caused by him to the victim and society and willingness on his part to repair that damage.

The victim-offender conflict of interests resolution is envisaged not to be limited to traditional administration of justice. The supporters of restorative justice wish to act hand in hand with Alternative Dispute Resolution Programmes. Two suggestions have been given in this respect.[21] *Firstly,* in view of new paradigm of restorative justice traditional system of criminal justice be replaced totally by establishing new system of dispute settlement ensuring rapid justice, and *secondly,* with a view to give the dominant role to be played by restorative justice old techniques should give way to new techniques and principles.

Restorative justice in its aims seems to be improvement upon the traditional criminal justice system. It aims to soften the attitude of both—offender and victim by means of reintegrating them in society. Gerry Johnstone summarises a number of benefits of restorative justice system over the traditional punishment system.

Firstly, it will ensure better position to victims by providing for meeting their needs. It is quite preferable to victims as traditional notion of satisfaction from punitive justice does not remain for long and does no material profit to victim. In restorative justice system victim feels greater satisfaction through restitution with healing effect.

Secondly, restorative justice benefits offender as it provides him a chance of mingling with society and relieving him from total seclusion. It also helps him in reforming by deterring from future criminality. Offender remains no more subjects of scorn and alienation. By mixing him with society the purpose of preventive and deterrent justice are served in a better way.

Thirdly, restorative justice benefits community by the way of real satisfaction of victim and offender so as to contribute in better way to society in positive manner. It ensure autonomy of both the offender and victim along with better relation between the two.

Fourthly, it reposes faith in administration justice and agencies responsible criminal justice get better support and co-operation from victim and offender both.

(C) Modes of Ensuring Restorative Justice to the Victims of The Crimes

The victim-oriented criminal justice system has inspired the proponent's restorative justice to vow that victim shall remain more "a forgotten man" under modern welfare society committed to secure justice to all the citizens. After commission of the crime restorative justice seeks to create non-violent social relationship in the community. It keeps a proper balance between the needs of the victim and also those of the offenders. Justice can be secured to a victim of crime either through restitution or compensation. Dr. Schafer made a survey of 29 countries and identified three classes of remedies to the victims through restitution or compensation.

1. *Damages*—civil in nature and awarded in civil proceedings.
2. *Restitution*—either civil in nature but awarded in criminal proceedings; and
3. *Compensation*—either civil in nature and awarded in criminal proceedings or neutral in nature and awarded through a special procedure.

It is becoming common feeling that public has become frustrated with the system of "Assembly in Justice." Through this system convicted criminals are placed on parole or probation and are left to commit further crimes[22], criminal sanction as deterrent becomes ineffective. In search of new sentencing options criminal law lawyers, criminologists and social reviewer suggest legislative measures to ensure restitution as a constructive alternative to the severity of imprisonment and the leniency of probation. It is suggested that restitutive justice should be adhered as the principal objective of criminal law. Under "restitutive justice" the offender is required to repay the victim from his own resources or from wages earned by the offender in the prison.

Many terms have been interchangeably used by criminal lawyers and criminologists so as to reflect the criminal-victim relationship. Thus, the terms reparation, restitution, composition and compensation are often used interchangeably. Though they do not represent the same view point. They differ basically in legal philosophy and very importantly in administration. The picture is not very much clear due to civil law nature of composition, criminal nature of restitution to victim and state responsibility to ensure security to all citizens and provide compensation when it fails to do so. Thus, the different terms may be explained as below:

1. *Composition*—it is outcome of the joint effort of the offender and victim by way of compounding the matter by the way of settlement. It may be either without the permission of the court or with the permission of court in compoundable cases between the parties.
2. *Reparation*—is obtained from the offender by the victim of the crime.
3. *Restitution*—is another form of reparation making offender to feel responsibility and provide reparation of loss of the victim and restoring him in better position by restoring rights damaged or destroyed by the offender. Restitution is penal in character and thus represents a correctional goal in the criminal case.
4. *Compensation*—views to counter-balance the loss resulting from the criminal act of the offender. It adds a new dimension in criminal-victim-society relationship. It indicates and involves the responsibility of the State.

From the point of view of victims rights enforcement and justice done to him justice may be divided into either restutional justice or compensative justice.[23]

(D) Restitutive Justice

Restitutive justice requires the offender to repay the victim. The etymological meaning of restitution is restoring any thing unjustly taken from another. It means putting thing in the same condition as it was before the criminal act of the offender. But it may be effective in very few categories of cases like victim of the crime of theft, extortion, kidnapping, etc. But in cases of heinious crimes like murder, rape and other like offences causing loss of life or dignity, physical or mental suffering, social stigma, outrage of modesty, etc. putting in the similar situation may not be possible. Therefore, in criminal administration of justice restitution has specific meaning of requiring convicted person to pay for crime to the victim. Restitution may be either monetary or cash restitution or service restitution. In monetary restitution offender is asked to make financial compensation to the victim. The service restitution requires performing certain works which will benefit the community at large. The monetary or cash restitution may be ordered by a criminal court either from the own resources of the victim or out of wages earned by the offender while undergoing the punishment of imprisonment under criminal justice system.

The obvious benefit of cash restitution is that it satisfies both—makes the offender responsible for what he has done and thereby is relieved from seclusion and it satisfies victim as wrong is righted. The service restitution gives solace to the society that it has received reparation from the offender.

Restitution awarded to victim has added benefit over the fine imposed on the offender as a punishment. Fine goes to the State coffer and leaves the victim unidentified for the loss of property or injuries suffered. On the other hand cash restitution goes directly to the victim who is benefited thereby.

The system of providing benefit to the victim's crime by the way restitution by the offender has many benefits. *Firstly,* the rationale of restitution relates to the damage done by the crime and crime itself. It arises from the worsen relationship created between the victim and the offender. *Secondly,* restitution is one of the number of competing objectives established for the offender. For example, it may take place of rehabilitation which is not very clear and sometimes misleading. *Thirdly,* restitution involves participation of offender in making good relations with victim as well as responsible member of society. *Fourthly,* it changes perception of society towards the offender. *Lastly,* restitution raises victim to his previous level. Howard Zehr has rightly summarised the position in the following words:

"Retribution seeks to right the balance by lowering the offender to the level to which the victim has been reduced. It tries to defeat the wrongdoer, annulling his or her claim to superiority and confirming the victim's sense of worth. Restitution, on the other hand, seeks to raise the victim to his or her previous level."[24]

It is submitted that the ideal explained in the above observation is sound and welcome. But restitutive justice is not altogether free from blemishes and shortcomings. The blemishes are pointed out by the critics of restitutions on following grounds:

(i) Restitution compensates victims. By nature it is civil rather than a criminal sanction. Therefore, it should not be ordered without a full civil trial.
The criticism based on strict separation between civil and criminal proceedings is not very much convincing in view of the modern view that civil and criminal law have the common objective. Restitution places focus on rehabitation, deterrence and retribution and thereby it becomes a criminal sanction.

(ii) The guilty person may be ordered to reimburse his victim only after a full trial on the question of damages. Adopting sentencing procedures to determine the amount of restitution procedural safeguards available to offender are violated. The offender is deprived of right to fair trial.
It is to be noted that barring a few cases relating to property loss, restitution is not sufficient recompense. The technicality of civil procedure need not put impediment in administration of criminal justice through restitution.

There are many shortcomings of restitution and the effectuation of restitution is not very easy. The following are barriers that directly influence successful restitution programmes:

1. Some justice professionals believe that restitution is simply uncollectible. In most cases offender may be too poor to pay the amount of restitution.
2. There is feeling that probation and parole officers are not collection agents.
3. Restitution programmes may fail to work well due to adequate funding agencies.
4. Restitution orders are often not in the priority of court ordered payments. They are followed behind the court costs, fines, costs of incarceration and other financial obligations.
5. It is not mandatory for the courts to order restitution. It is discretionary and may not be ordered consistently in case of—
   (i) Determination of payment schedule;
   (ii) Order of restitution;
   (iii) Monitoring and enforcement of restitution orders;
   (iv) Imposition of restitution conditions following period of incarceration;
   (v) Application of sanction for non-payment;
   (vi) Collection of restitution payments;
   (vii) Amendment of payment schedules; and
   (viii) Distribution of funds to victims.

In spite of certain shortcomings restitution is a progressive measure to console the victim and save him from permanent ruin. The rationality of restitution has been very well elaborated by Task Force on Victims of Crime appointed by President Reagan which submitted its final report in 1982. The report reads:

> "It is simply unfair that victims should have to liquidate their assets, mortgage their home or sacrifice their health or education or that of their children while the offender escape responsibility for the financial hardship he has imposed ... The victim may be placed in a financial crises that will last a life time. If one of the two must go into debt, the offender should do so."[25]

Restitutive justice may seem punitive but it serves compensatory goals. It serves two purposes. *Firstly,* it provides victim satisfaction that criminal law seeks to prevent private revenge. *Secondly,* punishment in proportion to harm is emotionally felt as "compensation" for the public damage done. As Stephen Schafer point out the compensatory aspect of restitution is logical expansion of the "symbolic" compensation already offered by criminal punishment.[26]

Though, the nature of payment of restitution appears to be of civil nature its place in criminal administration of justice is well recognised as rehabilitative, deterrent, retributive and so on. It should be made clear that restitution operates in criminal justice system but the victim at best occupies a second role. There is no formal recognition of the fact that the crime was committed against an individual who has suffered the harm as a result. Still criminal justice is primarily designed to control crime through punishing the offender. Therefore, as Harland and Rosen pointed out in 1990, restitution is an "inherent tension that arises when efforts are made to use the criminal law, with focus on vindication of society's interests in punishing offenders, to reimburse victim for the harm done them by specific offenders."

(E) Compensative or Compensatory Justice

The restitutive justice putting main emphasis on the responsibility of the offender to restore victim in earlier position may not be very successful due to bad economic condition of the offender. This practical problem faced by restitution as effective measure to do justice with the victims thinking developed that insurance-based programmes should be launched by public agency which could make direct payment to the victim.

In ordinary parlance the expression means making things equivalent; satisfying or making amends for loss, recompense or remuneration or pay.[27] In early times states encouraged compensation to victims but in the present time reimbursement of the victim or of his family by the victimiser is not common. As a matter of fact both the concepts of compensation and restitution have been understood interchangeably. Viewed from this angle, compensation is the counter-balancing of the victim's suffering and loss that results from the wrongful act of the offender. It indicates societal responsibility and represents a non-criminal purpose.

Compensatory justice resembles to restitutive justice in one form. Compensatory justice has two aspects. The first aspect of compensatory justice is that offender must be legally asked to compensate the victims. It is restitutive in nature as it provides financial restitution. But the situations may arise wherein offender may not be in a position nor would it be feasible for administrative system to ask the offender to compensate the victim. There are many offences where offenders are not identified nor apprehended nor convicted. In such a situation problem posed is; should be victim be left unredressed? If so be, it will frustrate the ends of criminal justice and victim will be forced to lead to secondary victimisation.

Viewed from this angle compensatory justice distinguishes compensation from restitution. Compensation here does not require the apprehension and conviction of an individual offender to provide financial relief to the victim. State takes the responsibility to securing justice to the victims. Victims of nearly every type of violence or abuse, including rape, assault, child abuse, domestic violence, etc. are eligible for financial help. Family members of homicide victims and sex abused child victims all need compensatory justice. In such type of compensatory justice state compensation programmes gather funds through relatively small assessment against all criminals and then distribute those funds to the victims who need help. On the other hand, restitution requires that criminal who injured a specific victim be ordered to reimburse the victim for the losses suffered by the victim. Thus, compensatory justice converts the personal responsibility of the offender into the liability of the state.

United States Senator Mike Mansfield while introducisng a Bill in the Senate to compensate the victims of crimes stated that, "the point has been reached where we must given consideration to the victim of the crime, i.e. to the one who suffers because of crime. For him society has failed miserably ... society has an obligation. When the protection of society is not sufficient to prevent a person from being victimised society then has the obligation to compensate the victim for that failure of protection."[28]

The compensatory justice should have the following considerations:

1. A compensation plan must be based on the conclusion that the government has failed in its responsibility of protecting its citizens from crime.
2. Compensation must be available to all victims of crime.
3. Compensation should include medical expenses, mental health counselling, lost wages for victims unable to work because of crime-related injury, lost support for dependents of homicide victims, funeral expenses, etc.
4. An effective compensation plan must provide for a speedy system of compensation.

Thus, compensatory justice requires payment of compensation to the victim by state. The rational behind this approach is understandable and appreciable in view of the modern social welfare concept of the state. The rationale behind State responsibility may be narrated as follow:

1. State's responsibility to compensate all the victims of the crimes is broadly based on social insurance.
2. Akin to social insurance policy there is plea of "shared risks." Like other type of dangers risk of crime victimisation should also be insured.
3. Government exists for providing security to all the citizens. If it fails to do so, it is responsibility of the state to provide compensation to the victims. In this respect observation of Mr. Justice Goldberg, a former Judge of the United States Supreme Court is very appropriate. He says: "the victim of robbery or an assault has been denied the protection of the law in a very real sense, and society should assume some responsibility for making him whole."[29]

4. The welfare concept of the modern state provides rationale for compensation victims of different types of contingencies.
5. The concept of welfare state also gives birth to the theory of "mercy of the government." The government is required to give *exgratia* compensation to the victims of crime, accident and natural calamities.[30]

Many countries of the world have recognised the responsibility of the State to compensate victims of the crimes. The rationale behind such recognition of State responsibility was very well summed by U.K. Minister of Home Affairs in 1964, when he said: "The intention is not that the State should be given the same liability for compensation as the offender, but that the State should go so far as is reasonable to ensure that the victim does not suffer undue hardship.[31]

(F) Assistance Programmes for the Victims

With the change of outlook towards the victims of the crimes and giving up their fate as 'forgotten man', the plea of justice to the victims short of restitution and compensation has got momentum. Assistance programmes make them feel that they are no more neglected men. They have every sympathy of the society. Assistance programmes may including informations intended to help them so as to cope with emotional, social and practical consequences of the crime.

The Assistance programmes in relations to the victims of the crimes may take the following forms:

1. Emergency help to meet immediate needs;
2. Continuing medical, psychological, social and material help;
3. Advice to prevent further victimization;
4. Legal aid and assistance during the criminal process; and
5. Assistance in obtaining reparation by the offender or other agencies or compensation from State.

The need of victim-oriented Criminal Justice system is attracting not only national concern but also the international concern. The study in the next chapter will be devoted to analyse how world wide move is getting momentum towards development of victim-oriental criminal justice system. In coming years criminal justice is bound to face more and more stresses due to increasing role of terrorist activities without any bound. In such activities victims are more badly affected for none of their fault except of the chance of their being present nearby place of occurrence.

Notes and References

1. *New Horizons in Criminology*, 3rd ed., 288.
2. Plato, *The Republic*, trans. A.D. Lindsay (Everyman's Library ed. 1950) Book IV.
3. Aristotle, the *Politics* trans. E. Barker (Oxfor 1946), Book III, 1282 b.
4. Ward, Lester F., *Applied Sociology* (Boston, 1906), p. 21.
5. Spencer, Herbert, *Justice* (New York), 1891, p. 46.
6. Aristotle, *The Nicomachean Ethics*, trans. H. Rackam (Loeb Classical Library ed. 1934) Book V, iii. 6.
7. *Ibid.*, Book V, iv.
8. *State of Gujarat* v. *Hon'ble Hight Court of Gujarat* (1998) 7 S.C.C. 392 at p. 406 (K.T. Thomas J.).
9. (1977) 3 S.C.C. 287.
10. *Ibid.*, pp. 289-90 (para 7).
11. Quoted from *Victims Restitution* by S.V. Joga Rao, *The Lawyer*, June 1990, p. 17.
12. (2004) 9 S.C.C. 37.
13. *Ibid.*, p. 47.
14. *State of M.P.* v. *Bala* (2005) 8 S.C.C.l; *Adu Ram* v. *Mukhna* (2005) 10 S.C.C. 597.
15. *State of U.P.* v. *Virendra Prasad* (2004) 9 S.C.C. 37 at p. 48.
16. Rao, S.V. Joga, *Victim Restitution, The Lawyer*, June 1990, p. 17.
17. Zender, Lucia, *Victim*: The Oxford Handbook of criminology (3rd ed.) Oxford University Press, pp. 444-47.
18. *Oxford Handbook of Criminology.*
19. Quoted from the Judgement of K.T. Thomas J. in *State of Gujarat* v. *Hon'ble High Court of Gujarat* (1998) 7 S.C.C. 392, 412.
20. Quoted from, Easton, Susan and Piper, Christie, *Sentencing and Punishment—The Quest for Justice*, Oxford University Press 157-58.
21. *Ibid.*, p. 158, see also Zender, Lucia, Victims—*Oxford Handbook of Criminology* (3rd edition), Oxford University Press, p. 446.

22. Mikva, Abner J., *Victimless Justice,* Journal of Criminal and Criminology (1980), pp. 189-90.
23. Das, Bharat B., The Victims in the Criminal Justice System (1997), p. 54.
24. Gerry Johnstone, *Restorative Justice: Ideas, Values Debates* (2002), p. 62.
25. The President's Task on *Victims of Crime: Final Report* (1982), p. 18.
26. Schafer, Stephen, *Victimology: The Victim and His Criminal,* Reuston Virginia (1977), p. 3.
27. Webster, *A Dictionary of the English Language*; also Jowitt, Earl, *The Dictionary of English Law,* Sweet and Maxwell, p. 434.
28. Culhane, California Enacts Legislation to Aid Victims of Criminal Violence, 18, *Stanford Law Rev.* (1965), p. 262.
29. Goldberg, Equality and Governmental Action 39, *New York University Review,* 224 (1974).
30. Rajan, V.N. *Victimology in India,* Allied Publishers, New Delhi (1981) pp. 7-9. Mr. Rajan has made elaborate study on the point and made out very valuable points relating to State responsibility to compensate the victims.
31. Alphonso, G.M., "Victim Compensation—A Conceptual Analysis", *Central India Law Quarterly,* Vol. II, 1998, p. 459.

4

Worldwide Trend Towards Realisation of the Victims' Rights

The study in the foregoing chapter established how the idea of victim oriented criminal justice system has inspired the ways and means of the redressal of hardships suffered by the victims of crime through restitution, compensation and assistance programmes. This theoretical acceptance of the victim-oriented justice has laid many efforts both at international and national levels in the different parts of the world.

The study in this chapter will be devoted to the identification and recognition of victims because the development of victimology as separate branch of study has made the concept of victims of the crimes more and more widened covering all sorts of victims of possible misfortunes arising out of traditional criminal acts and new criminal activities like terrorist activities and atrocities and abuse of powers. The study in this chapter also make an endeavour to point out how victim-oriented criminal justice system has got recognition of the world community through United Nations. Efforts will also be made to discuss how European communities and common law and civil law countries have made efforts to establish the rights of the victims of the crimes.

I. WIDENING CONCEPT OF VICTIM

The term victim did not attract much of research under the traditional work of criminologists. It attracted serious thought after the end of the second world war when victimology came to be discussed as a crime relating to victims. The term 'victim' is one of moral approbation. It lacks descriptive percesion in respect of actual human behaviour. Webster dictionary defines 'victim' as the person who is acted upon and usually adversely affected by a force agent.[1] Oxford English Dictionary gives the definition of 'victim' by way of inclusion of certain categories of persons. According to it (i) victim is a person who is put to death or subjected to misfortune by another; (ii) one who suffers severally in body or property through cruel or oppressive treatment; (iii) one who is reduced or destined to suffer under some oppressive or destructive agency; and (iv) one who perishes or suffers in health, etc. from some enterprise or pursuit voluntarily undertaken. In a weaker sense, one who suffers from some injury, hardship or loss, is badly treated or taken advantage of, etc."[2] The dictionary meaning of the term victim are value laden interpretation in relation to the definition of adversity, oppression and suffering.[3]

Bharat B. Das has very aptly pointed out that the word 'victim' may be attributed five fundamental factors,[4] namely, nature, society, energy supply, motorization and criminality. The factor of nature plays its role by causing disasters such as earthquake, flood, droughts and famine. The society factor holds a collective potential for starting mass conflict that may generate genocide, terrorism and abuse of powers. Among other aspects of socially determined victimity are the consequences of over population, poverty, illiteracy, alcoholism, drug addiction, prostitution and occupational diseases. Motorisation and energy resources are causing innumerable traffic accidents on land, at sea, and in the air, apart from industrial and domestic accidents. Above all are the victims of crimes. The glimpse at the field of victimology reveals two types of victims. The first type consists of direct victims, i.e. those who are alive and suffering on account of the harm inflicted by the offender while committing crime.

The second type comprises of indirect victims who are dependants of the direct victims of crimes who undergo sufferings due to deprivation of their bread winner. A direct victim is a person who has suffered direct physical, psychological, reputational or pecuniary harm as a result of the commission of crime.

United Nations Declaration of Basic Principles of Justice for Victims and Abuse of Power defines victim in very wide terminology so as to include both direct and indirect victims. The General Assembly Resolution 40/34 (1985) realised that million of people throughout the world suffer harm as a result of crime and abuse of power and that the rights of these victims have not been adequately recognized. It also realized that the victims of crime and the victims of abuse of power, and also frequently their families, witnesses and others who aid them, are unjustly subjected to loss, damage or injury and that they may, in addition, suffer hardship when assisting in prosecution of offender. It defines victim as follow:

> "(1) Victims mean who, individually or collectively, have suffered harm including physical or mental injury, emotional suffering, economic loss or substantial impairment of their fundamental right, thorough acts or omission that are in violation of criminal laws operative within Member States including those laws proscribing criminal abuse of power. A person may be considered a victim, under this Declaration, regardless of whether the perpetrator is identified, apprehended, prosecuted or convicted and regardless of the familiar relationship between the perpetrator and the victim. The term victim also includes, where appropriate, immediate family or dependent of the direct victim and persons who have suffered harm in intervening to assist victims in distress or to prevent victimization."

In addition, U.N. Declaration extends the scope of victims by defining the victims of abuse of power to include persons who, individually or collectively, have suffered harm, including physical or mental injury, emotional suffering, economic loss or substantial impairment of their fundamental rights, through acts or omissions that do not yet constitute violation of national criminal laws but of internationally recognized norms relating human rights.

The definition of United Nations General Assembly Declaration was further elaborated as to the types—harm, injury, loss of damage caused by wrongful conduct by the United Nations Social Council's draft Guidelines for Measures on behalf of Victims of Crime and Abuse of Power. It includes "the loss of life or of support, impairment of health, including physical or psychological injury, pain and suffering both physical and mental, loss of liberty, loss of income or livelihood, loss of property or damage to it which is not subject to restitution and deprivation of the use of property. Due account must also be taken of the special damages or expenses and costs reasonably incurred by the victim or, where appropriate, by the victim's family, dependants or heir, which resulted from the victimization including medical costs, transportation costs, funeral or burial costs and similar related costs and expenses.

The definition of victim in victimological perspective includes a wide range of victims. Victims may belong to the following categories:

1. Victims of War
2. Victims of accidents that occur:
   (a) on road,
   (b) on Railways,
   (c) on Aircrafts,
   (d) on Sea, and
   (e) on the Workplace.
3. Victims of the abuse of power by lawful authority:
   (a) Custodial death;
   (b) Death due police firing;
   (c) Groundless arrest or detention;
   (d) Unnecessary harassment; and
   (e) Police encounters.
4. Victims of rape and other offences.
   A number of victims may fall prey of offences of different kinds, e.g. victims of criminal conspiracy,

offences of giving or fabricating false evidence, fabricating false documents, certificates or causing disappearance of evidence by way of destruction or concealment of the documents, fraudulent acts with the intention of causing bodily or mental harm to a person, murder, miscarriage, hurt, wrongful restraint and wrongful confinement, assault, use of criminal force, kidnapping, abduction, forced labour, unnatural offence, theft, extortion, robbery and dacoit, cheating, mischief, arson, criminal trespass, adultery, bigamy, fraudulent marriage, dowry torture and death, defamation, criminal intimidation, insult and annoyance.

5. Victims of offences relating to manufacture and sale of adulterated, substandard and prohibited drugs, liquor and food.
6. Victims of offences of smuggling, black-marketing, unfair trade practice and evasion of tax.
7. Victim of offences committed by public servants, such as negligence and inefficiency in discharging their duties, corruption, bribery and misappropriation of public funds.
8. Victims of environmental pollution and wanton destruction of flora and fauna and public nuisance.
9. Victims of offences committed in the election.
10. Victims who are also offenders or perpetrators of crimes such as drunkenness, consumption of narcotic drugs, gambling, attempt to commit suicide and prostitution, which are otherwise known as victimless crimes.
11. Victims who create a compelling situation is which the offender reacts violently by committing a criminal act. Sometimes the victim provokes the offender to commit the crime, victims of affray, free fight and rioting may also be included in this category.
12. Victims of the criminal justice system or law enforcement agency—victimisation resulting from

the mal-administration of the criminal justice is not uncommon for legal systems. Individuals being so victimized may be called the victims of law and justice. They include accused/offenders or under trial prisoners and even convicted prisoners, witness including complainant and/or informant of a criminal case.

The wide-range recognition of victims has also contributed towards expanding expectations of victim who need protection in case of crimes against person, against property and against reputation. Victims of crime need psychological adjustment and compensation for the loss. Since victims experience considerable disruption of psychological, emotional cognitive and behavioural functions, they have to be given receptive years and rehabilitative measures. Victims also expect compensation for the loss suffered by them. The loss may be physical or property loss. The loss may be compensated through damages through filing a civil suit but it may receive due recognition in criminal justice system also. He may also receive compensation which is civil in nature but may be awarded by the criminal court which tries the case of the victim. Compensation may be ordered either against the employer or against the State.

2. REDRESSAL OF VICTIM'S GRIEVANCE UNDER UNITED NATIONS DECLARATION

The victim's of crime have got very favourable response at international plane. On November 29, 1985, the General Assembly of the United Nations adopted the Basic Prchisples of Justice for victims of crime and Abuse of Power. It expresses international concern with societal responses to the needs of victims. It establishes standard for access to justice requiring compassional treatment with due respect and dignity. Victims are also envisaged to have fair treatment by being informed of their rights, being informed of their role in criminal justice system; allowing their views about victims, proper legal assistance being given to them; by providing safety to victims as well as their family members by avoidance of unnecessary delay in the disposition of cases and the execution orders or decrees granting awards to victims.

The United Nations Declaration provides for three types of redressal to victim's grievances by the way of restitution, compensation and assistance.

(i) Restitution

(1) Offenders or third parties responsible for their behaviour should, where appropriate, make fair restitution to victims, their families or dependants. Such restitution should include the return of property or payment for the harm or loss suffered, reimbursement of expenses of services and restoration of rights.

(2) Governments should review their practices, regulations and laws to consider restitution as an available sentencing option in criminal cases, in addition to other criminal sanctions.

(3) In cases of substantial harm to the environment, restitution, if ordered, should include, as far as possible, restoration of the environment, reconstruction of the infrastructure, replacement of community facilities and reimbursement of the expenses of relocation, where such harm results in the dislocation of a community.

(4) Where public officials or other agents acting in an official or quasi-official capacity have violated national criminal laws, the victims should receive restitution from the State whose officials or agents were responsible for the Government under whose authority the victimizing act or omission occurred is not longer in existence. The State of Government successor in title should provide restitution to the victims.

(ii) Compensation

In addition to restitution United Nations Declaration provides for compensation to the victims of crime.

Compensation covers the following situations:

(i) When compensation is not fully available from the offender or other sources, States should endeavour to provide financial compensation to:

(a) Victims who have sustained significant bodily injury or impairment of physical or mental health as a result of serious crimes; and

(b) The family, in particular dependants of persons who have died or become physically or mentally incapacitated as a result of such victimization.

(ii) The establishment, strengthening and expansion of national funds for compensation to victims should be encouraged. Where appropriate, other funds may also be established for the purpose, including those cases where the State of which the victim is a national is not in a position to compensate the victim for the harm.

The Declaration did not limit remedies only to restitution or compensation it provided for a number of assistance with a view to make the victim actual participator in criminal justice process without any feeling of seclusion or dejection.

(iii) Assistance

(i) Victims should receive the necessary material, medical, psychological and social assistance through government, voluntary, community-based and indigenous means;

(ii) Victims should be informed of the availability of health and social services and other relevant assistance and readily afforded access to them.

(iii) Police, justice, health, social service and other personnel concerned should receive training to sensitize them to the needs of victims and guidelines to ensure proper and prompt aid.

(iv) In providing services and assistance to victims attention should be given to those who have special needs because of the nature of the harm inflicted or because of factors such as those, relating to race, colour, sex, age, language, religion, nationality, political or other opinion, cultural beliefs or practices, property, birth or family status, ethnic or social origin and disability.

As a matter of fact the vide range of remedies covered by U.N. Declaration is culmination of the victim oriented thinking from the start of the Universal Declaration of Human Rights, 1948. Section 18 of the Declaration spoke of the right of an effective remedy given to everyone. The some idea was reiterated under International Covenant on Civil and Political Rights by recognising the right of effective remedy in cases of violation of freedom even if such violation was committed by persons acting in an official capacity.

3. RECOGNITION OF VICTIMS' RIGHT IN EUROPEAN COMMUNITY

European Convention for the Protection of Human Rights and Fundamental Freedom provides for the enforceable right to compensation. Fair and adequate compensation along with rehabilitation is aim of Article 14(1) of the Convention on Torture and other Cruel, Inhuman or Degrading Treatment or Punishment. It states, "each state party shall ensure in its legal system that the victims of an act of torture obtains readiness and has an enforceable right to fair and adequate compensation, including the means for as full rehabilitation as possible. In the event of death of the victim as a result of an act of torture, his dependents shall be entitled to compensation."

In March 1981, The European Committee on Crime Problems of Council of Europe constituted a select committee of experts on victim and criminal and social policy. Its recommendations were approved by the Council of Ministers of the Council of Europe on June 28, 1985. The main recommendations[5] included that—

1. A victims of crime who addressed his grievance to the police should be treated in such a way as to avoid further emotional damage. He should be informed of different available facilities from public and private organisations. It also included information about suggested restitutional claim. The claim could be made against the offender and in certain cases against the State.
2. Public prosecutor should see that offender has made restitution to the victim and if necessary proceeding to be launched against the offender.
3. Throughout the proceeding victims position was to be recognised with dignity.
4. The victim should be given role in inflicting penal sanction upon the offender.
5. Restitution should have the top priority.
6. Offender to be given chance to earn money to provide restitution to the victim. Thus, by way socialisation and creative restitution victim was to be compensated.
7. The special feature of the recommendation was that the criminal courts were given inherent power to impose restitution order on the offender as a separate sanction. Victim was also to be informed about filing the compensatory claim against the offender.
8. In order to ensure effective realisation of compensation from the offender it was to be executed in the same way as fines.
9. An encouragement for informal settlement between the victim and the offender without involving the formal criminal procedure was to be preferred.

4. MEASURES ENSURING JUSTICE TO VICTIMS IN COMMON LAW SYSTEM

Under the common countries/Anglo-Saxan Jurisprudence accusatorial system of trial prevails and victim or state representing society develops a private vengeance.

Criminal trial is a contest between the accuser and the accused and judge stands as a referee. Typically the proceeding takes place publicly and orally and is not proceeded by any official investigation or preparation of evidence. Historically offender gained better treatment under accusatorial system as he could not be punished unless crime against him was proved beyond reasonable doubt. On the other hand, under inquisitorial system there is elimination of the figure of private accuser and appropriation of that role by public officials. The second thing was that judge did not remain impartial referee. He became active inquisor who was forced to seek evidence and control the nature and objective of inquiry. Contest was between individual and state. Historically inquisitorial proceedings had tended to be secret and written rather than public and oral. Typical criminal proceeding was divided into three basic parts: the investigative phase, the examining phase and the trial. The inquisitorial system was more victims-oriented who could have say and control the trial by active participation.[6]

After experience of the shortcomings of the trial procedure the common countries show a trend of shift from accusatorial system to inquisitorial system and inquisitorial procedure has learned much from the accusatorial system. In view of human rights development both systems have taken care of the rights of the victims. The following position given in different systems will be informative of the new trends of victim-oriented criminal justice in different countries.

(i) Measures of Providing Justice to Victims in U.S.A.

America has taken lead in recognizing and enforcing victim's right. During the year 1960s and 1970s a moment started in American States in view of extraordinary rise of crime. It attracted Presidential interest to study through commission the growth of 'crime', 'riot' and 'violence'. Carolina took lead by enacting the victim compensation law. Other states followed the suit. In 1982 The President's Task Force on victims of crime recommended the routine imposition of restitution in criminal case with documented financial loss to victim. The recommendation of the President's Task Force formed basis of enacting Federal

Victims and Witnesses Protection Act, 1982. The distinguishing features of the Act were that—

(i) It required that report on the result of investigation submitted by the public prosecutor to the courts must contain 'Victim's Impact Assessment' in which Victim's point of view was to be given the prominence as to crime and its consequences. It had to narrate all sorts of losses suffered by the victim.

(ii) An attempt was made to enforce restitution ideologically and practically in Federal criminal process. The court could order restitution of damage caused to the victim as an independent penal sanction. The court could order restitution in addition to or in lieu of any other penalty authorised by the law.[7]

(iii) A shift in emphasis was changed. In all cases criminal procedure was expected to tend to restoration of peace through restitution between the offender and the victim and not between offender and the state.

(iv) A shift in priority was also emphasized. The aim of restitution was to act as a means of reparation to victims rather than as a technique for rehabilitating the offender. It required just restitution in proportion to loss or injury.

(v) It proposed that restitution should have priority in the criminal justice system and it should have upper hand in comparison to traditional punitive sanction of imprisonment and fine.[8]

Thus, the victim was assured of fair treatment in Federal Criminal Justice system, was assured of his participation in process and protection from victimization along with restitution on priority basis.

The earlier referred Act was followed by the enactment of the Victims of Crime Act, 1984. By enacting it Congress provided funding for victims assistance, victim compensation and training and technical assistance for victim service providers across the nation. Its innovative funding mechanism consisted of fines, penalties and bond forfeiture. The victims of federal crimes were made eligible for state compensation benefits. States responded so by making necessary amendments in their respective laws.

The Crime Control Act of 1990 made effective the Victim's Rights Restitution Act, 1990, created a Federal Crime Victim's Bill of Rights including a number of rights. Victims were assured of fair treatment, dignity and privacy, reasonable protection from accused/offender; right to be notified of court proceedings, right to participation, right of information about the conviction, sentencing, imprisonment and release of the offender and above all the right of restitution.

The Violence Against Women Act, 1994 as a part of the *Violent Crime Control and Law Enforcement Act, 1994* identified particular crimes subject to mandatory restitution. It departed from the earlier-trend of courts' discretionary ordering of restitution and very clearly stated that conviction for four types of crimes must include mandatory restitution as part of an offender's punishment. The four types of offences relate to:

1. Domestic violence;
2. Sexual assault;
3. Sexually exploited and other Abused Children; and
4. Telemarketing fraud.

The Act also listed expenses for which victim restitution was required. It included (1) Lost income; (2) Necessary Child Care; (3) Transportation; (4) Other expenses related to participation in the investigation or prosecution of the offence; and (5) Attendance at proceeding related to an offence.

The Mandatory Restitution Act, 1996 (Title II of the Anti-terrorism and Effective Death Penalty Act of 1996) required federal judges to order full restitution from offenders who have been committed or pled guilty to specific charges of—

(i) Fraud,
(ii) Property Crimes,
(iii) Consumer Product Tempering, and
(iv) Drug Crimes.

In 1995 Attorney General Guide lines for Victim and Witnesses was issued to include, information and referral; Protection from intimidation and harassment; Consultation and notice; Secure waiting areas; Return of property held as evidence; Payment of forensic rape exam; Notice and payment for testing and counselling for sexually transmitted diseases; Custodial released eligibility information, Allocation and Victim impact statements to the Court, and Restitution.

It required that restitution order should be enforced by all available means, i.e. all benefits provided to the dependent by federal agency must be suspended until the defendant made a "good faith" effort to pay restitution order was established as a condition of probation or supervised release. By amending the Victims Right and Restitution Act, 1990 it was made essential that if Court did not order restitution or only partial restitution it had to record reasons for doing so.

In addition to restitution American States have followed victims' compensation scheme. It is usually denied to family members of offender in order to prevent "unjust environment" of criminal. In cases of contributory victimization, compensation to victim is to be reduced proportionately. Few States provide compensation to non-state victims too.[9] Compensation scheme is followed by a number of verification and investigation. It includes—scanning of police report, offender-victim relationship and scrutiny of hospital records, perusal of insurance documents, payment available under insurance schemes, Workmen's compensation scheme, etc., employment of victim, personal finances of victim, outcome of prosecution, etc. Compensation is payable where victim is not restituted from the money collected from the offender as restitution orders are enforced or collected. In such a situation tax payer's money is to be utilized or small sum is collected from all criminals and then such fund is utilized for victim who needs. Therefore it is used cautiously. The objectives of victim compensation programmes in the United States are:

1. to demonstrate the State's concern for the plight of the crime victim;
2. to reduce or eliminate the financial suffering caused by the criminal injury on the innocent victims of crime and their dependents;
3. to improve community crime prevention and better support for the criminal justice system through increased public cooperation; and
4. to contain and limit the expenditure on this account.

A new trend in America is to give statutory basis to victims right of participation in proceedings at all crucial stages including the sentencing proceeding. By now thirty two states have chosen to include such a provision in their Constitution. Other States have made statutory provisions. Senate has proposed such amendment to be incorporated in the Constitution but it has not got congressional approval.

(ii) Measures taken for Providing Justice to the Victims in the United Kingdom

In United Kingdom criminal inquiries compensation was introduced for the first time in 1964 on a non-statutory basis to provide *ex-gratia* compensation to the victims of crimes of violence and to those hurt in their attempts to arrest the offender or to prevent crimes. Under criminal Injuries Compensation Scheme 1964 the scheme was administered by an independent Criminal Injuries Board consisting of a Chairman with wide legal experience and some lawyers who practise in the courts. Although members of Board were appointed by Ministers and Government was responsible for providing money, decision of Board was independent and uninfluenced by the Government. The Board was transformed into a statutory body under the Criminal Justice Act of 1988.

In 1972 Criminal Justice Act accepted the payment of compensation as an appropriate action after criminal conviction. It was largely replaced by the Criminal Court Act,

1973. It was subsequently amended many times and lastly was replaced by the Criminal Justice Act of 1988.

The Criminal Act of 1973 empowered Court to make compensation order by or before which a person was convicted of an offence.[10] This order was in addition any other order thought to be appropriate by the Court and it could be made irrespective of an application of the victim. There was no need of application by the victim. It was awarded in cases of personal injury, loss or damage resulting from the offence.[11] The move of the Court to award compensation in cases of damage suffered by victims was approved by Scarman L.J. in *R.* v. *Inwood*[12] by making clear that it was a convenient and rapid means of avoiding the expenses of civil litigation. However, while awarding compensation causal link between the offence and loss suffered by the victim was to be found, though the complete causation was not insisted upon and it was thought judicially sufficient if loss or damage could fairly be said to have resulted from the offence.[13] Certain points were clear—

1. Victim had not to apply. The Court could itself award compensation.
2. Some causal link between offence and loss suffered by victim was essential.
3. Compensation order was not punitive but the sum awarded was purely by the way of compensation.
4. Compensation should explicitly refer to loss suffered.[14]
5. Offender's financial capacity or means to pay compensation was to be taken into consideration.[15]
6. There were certain schemes which provided for compensation to the victim from State.

Many schemes relating to 'Victim Support' and Victim's Welfare were launched with a view to providing victim right to be heard; necessary information to protect his interest; right to be protected by law enforcement agencies; right to receive compensation and restitution; right to receive support and assistance, pecuniary and financial support, etc. Home office issued charter as Victim's Charter, 1990 and Victim's

Carter, 1996 providing for standards of service to the given to the victim and his family. It included right to be treated with human dignity and respect; right to support and protection; right to compensation and reparation. Criminal Justice Act, 1988 made order to compensation necessary in certain cases like the case of death, loss or damage. In case of making no order of compensation a duty was imposed on the Court to give reasons for not doing so. The Criminal Justice Act, 2003 finally provides as follows:[16]

1. As regards to compensation award power of Magistrate's Court is limited up to 5,000 pounds but there is no limit in the Crown's Court.
2. A compensation order can be instead of any other disposal or punishment.
3. Courts must give reason if they are not imposing a compensation order.

Compensation was also awarded through the State Funded Criminal Injuries Schemes. It was noted earlier scheme which started in 1964 was modified many times (1969, 1979, 1990 and 1995). Finally, Criminal Injury Compensation Act, 1995 established a 'new tariff' approach based on types of injuries rather than individualised consideration of harm or damage. It grouped injuries comparable to severity into twenty-five bands, each receiving a standard fixed payment from 1,000 to 2,50,000 pounds.[17]

The other mode of doing justice was reparation. The statutory basis of reparation order can be found under The Crime and Disorder Act, 1998, The Youth Justice and Criminal Evidence Act, 1999 and Power of Criminal Court Act, 2000. Reparation scheme could be implemented at three different levels in the criminal justice system. It could be applied at pre-prosecution stage so as to divert offender from prosecution. It could be applied at the stage between conviction and sentence. It could be applied at third stage as a part of punishment so as to make offender personally responsible for his behaviour. It could inspire and rehabilitate him by mixing with victim and other members of the society.

The victims are getting more and more informational

right as to progress of the case. Victim is also receiving active right of participation in prosecution as witness. Victim's charter of 1996 allows a victim an influential say in sentencing. His personal statement of victim or giving him opportunity to participate in sentencing process is a real innovation. The narration of facts, statement of physical, financial, psychological, social or emotional effects of the offence on victim and his family may affect prosecution, bail on sentencing decision. However, governmental guidance issued in 1996 makes it optional and not primarily a sentencing tool. He has no right to give a statement in person.

There appears to be some difference on this point between the U.K. practice and that of the practice prevailing in U.S.A. where victims are given some say over sentence or an influential say in sentencing.[18] The following conditions must be fulfilled for making a victim eligible to receive compensation of the United Kingdom.

1. There must have been a prosecution regarding the offence against the victim. Exceptions can be allowed only for practical, technical and other good reasons.
2. Injury must be of such a nature as would entitle the victim to a damage of at least five hundred pounds.
3. When victim and offender happen to be of the same family, the Board must be satisfied that there was no likelihood of their living together and that they stopped living together before the application was made for compensation.
4. In the case of victim or the person claiming compensation on his behalf is of age less than 18 years. Compensation is to be paid only if the Board is satisfied that it would not be against the interest of the minor to make a full or reduced award.
5. There is no compensation payable in property offences.

5. MEASURES TAKEN FOR PROVIDING JUSTICE TO VICTIM IN CIVIL LAW COUNTRIES

Civil law countries like France and Germany with inquisitorial procedure of criminal justice have been providing better say to the victims of Crime. France takes lead in civil law countries. France and Germany take lead in victim's right of participation in the prosecution or to present civil claims within the criminal process.

(a) Measures of Compensation in France

In France The French Code of Criminal Procedure and the Act No. 77-5 of 1977 apply through out the country. When legislation was being framed and debated in 1975 and 1976 the position relating to compensation to the victims in other European countries was taken into account. The intention of the code was that community as a whole should accept an obligation towards the victims of offences which endanger life or physical well being. The Act No. 77-5 of 1977 came into force on January 3, 1977. It guaranteed State compensation for certain categories of physical injuries resulting from crime.

The distinguishing features the French law are follow:

(i) Victim's Right to Participate in the Prosecution

The French code of criminal procedure allows victim to join the prosecution as a matter of right. He can join in the criminal proceeding of prosecuting the offender, as a third party. Victims participation is material. He does not act only as a spectating witness.

(ii) Right to Complete Restoration of the Material Loss Caused by the Offender

The state provides for compensation to the victim even the accused is not prosecuted or convicted or is incapable of committing crime by reason of insanity or other legal infirmity. But apart from State compensation to victim of crime victim may combine his claim for compensation—*action civile*—in the criminal proceedings. The claim of victim was heard against the offender along with criminal case. It also allows complete restoration of material loss caused by the offender. The main idea behind restitution is that as far as possible, the injured party should be put back into the position which he occupied before the offence had taken place.

(iii) Non-National Treated on par with Nationals for the Payment of Compensation

A victim was entitled to compensation irrespective of the offender being prosecuted or convicted or not. The victims who were not French citizens were also entitled to be compensated in the same way as the French nationals.

(iv) Right of Victim to Claim Compensation against the State

There is guarantee of State compensation in certain class of victims of crimes. The community as a whole accepts an obligation towards the victims of offences which endanger life or physical well-being.

Since public fund is to be utilized for payment of compensation, the payment of compensation was subject to certain conditions. *First,* the cause of injury, loss or damages should result from wilful or involuntary acts which have the material features of an offence. *Secondly,* the Act envisages two types of consequences of crime. Injury resulting from offences must be physical. The result of offence must have resulted either in death or permanent disablement, or in total incapacity for work exceeding one month. The harm resulting from bodily injury must enrol financial loss, i.e. a loss or reduction of income, an increase in expenses or unfitness to carry on an occupation. *Thirdly,* a victim may be compensated only if he has no other right to compensation and is suffering economic hardships. *Fourthly,* behaviour of victim could also mitigate his chance of compensation. Compensation may be refused or reduced by reason of the injured party's behaviour at the time of the offence or relations with the perpetrator of the offence.

(v) Dependant's Right to Reparation and Compensation

In cases of the death of victim his dependents are personally entitled to reparation are also entitled to compensation provided they are undergoing serious hardships economically and there legal rights cannot be enforced effectively.[19]

(b) Justice to Victims of Crimes in the Federal Republic of Germany

French system of providing compensation to the victims of crimes finds place in Germany too of course with some variations. In Germany 'damages' comprised both 'restitution in kind' and 'monetary compensation'.

In May 1974, the Federal Government circulated a draft law on compensation for victims of crimes of violence. The draft was adopted by both the Houses of Parliament. The Act was promulgated in May 1976 and came into force on May 16, 1976. It governed law relating to compensation for victims of crime of violence. Under this Act anybody who had suffered damage to his health due to a crime of violence could claim compensation under Federal Welfare Act and Welfare benefit of compensation was available to him for the damage to health or economic loss. Like French ideology the law envisages that community has a special responsibility of security and saving people from becoming victims of crime of violence.[20] The Act envisages two types of victims—Direct Victims who survives after the violence and indirect victims who are dependents of the victim who lost life due to violence. The Act provides for both. It is designed to give adequate compensation to those who have become victim of such crime and the dependents of the dead victims. The advantages is that dependant should be freed atleast from the financial worries created by the loss of their bread-winner.

The Act provides that upon application, the victim of a crime of violence and his survivors may be paid compensation for damages to his health or pecuniary loss suffered as a result of that crime according to the Federal War Victims Maintenance Act which is applicable with necessary amendments and adaptations. This makes clear victims of crime of violence are treated like was victims and are entitled to the same benefits. In this way the victims compensation has been integrated into the framework of the social security system.

An exhaustive provision is made in Germany in the form of The Victim Protection Act. It was enacted on April 1, 1987. It was enacted for improving the position of the injured party. The object of the Act was to regulate three problematic issues.[21]

(i) It tried to improve the protection of the personality of the victim and other parties involved in the trial.

(ii) It newly regulated and improved the victims possibility of participating in criminal trial by giving it a statutory colour.

(iii) It extended the possibilities of obtaining restitution from the offender.

As to the first issue it provided that personal privacy connected question could be put before the victim/witness only when it was absolutely necessary to determine the truth. *Secondly,* victim/witness was to be interrogated by the court in absence of the defendants, if it could have affect on victim.[22]

As to the second issue with a view to provide stronger protection to the personality of victim public could be excluded during trial on the motion of the victim. Victims' right-of participation in criminal justice system has been ensured by the Victim Protection Act, 1987 in two ways:

(i) All persons who are victims of personal injuries by a crime shall be entitled to appear as joint plaintiffs besides the public prosecutor in the criminal trial. This includes, for example, persons who have become victim, of rape, kidnapping or attempted homicides and like cases.

(ii) Victims who are not entitled to appear as joint plaintiffs are also granted with certain minimal rights:

   (i) Right to be informed about the outcome of the court trial so far as they are affected.

   (ii) Right to have counsel for the protection of their right.

(iii) Right to file restitution claim against the offender within the criminal trial.[23]

Since the compensation to victim is regarded as a social security measure to be paid out of public exchequer, compensation is awarded with certain conditions. *Firstly*, compensation claim can be entertained only if crime is committed in Federal Republic or on its ship or on aeroplane. *Secondly*, claim of compensation can be entertained only if the claimant has suffered from crime of violence like intentional poison, act of putting public life in danger e.g. arson or a bomb; attack. *Thirdly*, victim will fail to obtain benefit if he was himself cause of his injury or some attributable behaviour. Thus, victim will succeed claim of compensation only if he is absolutely innocent victim of crime.[24]

However, the victim or his survivor dependent will be given compensation regardless of whether the offender is identified or convicted.

(c) Measures to Provide Justice to Victims in Italy

In Italy compensation for damages arising out of a criminal act is contained in Article 185 of the Penal Code. It provides that a criminal act causing damage of a patrimonial or non-patrimonial nature has to be compensated by the guilty person. The loss caused by criminal act will be assessed according to the civil law.

In cases of accidental injuries caused by motor vehicles, there is compulsory insurance scheme for civil liability.[25]

The fund is given from insurance companies equal to a percentage of the premium collected for each insurance contract and is designed to pay damages in the following cases:

(i) where the accident was caused by unidentified vehicle or boat,
(ii) where vehicle or boat was not insured, and
(iii) where vehicle or boat was insured by an Italian insurance policy with a company which at the time of the accident was being compulsorily wound up and declared insolvent.

In such cases the Ministry of Justice has under sideration a legislation ensuring responsibility of State for the payment of damages arising out of a crime, irrespective of the ultimate civil or criminal liability of the wrong doer.

(d) Compensatory Justice to the Victims of Crime in Netherlands

Around 1970 Netherlands thought to establish a compensation fund. The compensation to the victims of serious crimes was to be paid from the government funds. It was provided for conformation in cases of sever bodily injury sustained as result of crime of violence. The compensation was to be paid to direct victims if they survived the crime of violence and also to victim's representatives if they died. In latter case relatives included the victims surviving espouse, the children, and parents financially dependent on the earnings of the victim. The amount of compensation was determined according to what was just and fair. Direct damages done were taken into account while determining the amount of compensation.

One distinguishing feature of the compensation scheme in Netherland is that it is not necessary for the crime to have been reported to the police. The claim of compensation is to be made within six months of the committal of the crime or death of the victim. Requests for compensation are made to an independent committee of five members. The order of the committee is appeal able before the Court of Appeal at Hague in the following cases:

(i) where compensation was refused, or
(ii) the amount awarded was to small that the committee had apparently not reached a fair decision.

(e) Compensation to the Victims of the Crimes in Norway

Like Netherland, Norway also provides for compensation from public funds for personal injuries caused by punishable acts. Regulations to this effect was adopted by a Royal Decree of 12 March, 1976.

The salient features of scheme are—

(1) Compensation is also payable if offence is committed in a state of insanity or unconsciousness or by a boy below 14 years of age, provided the act is punishable under law.
(2) In case of death of the victim, compensation is awarded to relation who at the time of the death of victim were wholly or partially supported by the dead victim.
(3) The compensation from public fund may be granted when injury is inflicted within the Kingdom of Norway or on board a Norwegian vessel, aircraft, etc.
(4) Compensation may be awarded to the victim's relative in the directly ascending and descending line.
(5) Compensation in cases of accident injuries arising out of motor vehicles may be given only if deliberate intention can be proved.[26]

(f) Compensation to the Victims of the Crimes in Sweden

In Sweden too compensation is awarded as *ex gratia* from the public funds. Such scheme is operative since 1971 with some modification done in 1974.

Application for compensation is to be made to the Ministry of Justice and the same is granted by the Government.

The award of compensation is made for personal injuries caused by crimes intentionally or negligently. The criminal act may be committed in Sweden or elsewhere against any person permanently resident in Sweden. Compensation in Sweden is awarded even in those cases where the offender is not known or due to youth or insanity cannot be prosecuted.

Compensation is awarded with wider spectrum so as to include loss of earnings as well as medical expenses for pain and sufferings.

(g) Restitutional Justice to the Victims of the Crimes in U.S.S.R.

Union of Soviet Socialist Republic adopts the provision

for restitution mainly from the offender. The Fundamentals of Criminal Court Procedure for U.S.S.R. and the Union Republic, 1958 defines victim as a person who has suffered moral, physical or material injury as the result of a crime.

Victim has right to initiate at the trial a civil action against the accused. Such action will be examined by the court simultaneously with the criminal trial. Victim or his representatives have right to adduce testimony, evidence, participate in investigation and appeal against sentence.

The duty is primarily imposed upon the offender to make amends for the harm caused. It has to be imposed as one of the supplementary punishment. Article 32 of code provides that execution of duty to make amends for the harms caused consists in—

(i) direct elimination by ones own resources of the harm caused, or

(ii) compensation with one's own means for material loss, or

(iii) public apology before the victim or members in group as directed by the Court, or

(iv) Restitution is done by offender to the victim by passing a sum of money or by service.

The U.S.S.R. method of punishment provides a direct reparation to be paid by the offender to the injured victim by compensation either in money, Labour or in kind, for the harm caused.

(h) Compensation Plan for the Victims of the Crimes in New South Wales

On January 1, 1968 New South Wales adopted the Criminal Injuries Compensation Act. It makes order of compensation to the victims of the crimes in two ways:

(1) When the offender is brought on trial, the Court, upon conviction may order payment of compensation to the victim by the offender.

(2) In the case the offender is unable to pay the

amount of compensation or is acquitted, the victims makes application to under Secretary who forwards the claim with his report to treasurers there is provision for *ex gratia* payments to the victims of unsolved crimes.

(i) Compensatory Justice to the Victims of the Crimes in Newzealand

A quite innovative and revolutionary stand is taken by Newzealand. It is first country of the world to establish a modern programme to compensate victims of crime.[27] Newzealand enacted the Criminal Injury Compensation Act, 1963 which came into force January 1, 1964. It has been subsequently amended in 1966, 1969 and 1971. The basic philosophy behind this law is "rather the community's duty towards those who suffer misfortune than the liability of the state for failing to prevent crime."[28]

The Newzealand programme under the Act includes compensation for both direct victims, i.e. who suffer injury like bodily harm, mental or bodily shock and indirect victims, i.e. dependents of the person killed by such criminal act. The Act also provides for constitution of Crime Compensation Tribunals to hear and decide claims. Newzealand plan is more extensive than its British counterpart as it expressly provides for pain and suffering. It also allows compensation to victims even if the offender is member of the victim's family. The tribunal's power to award compensation is discretionary. In its discretion the tribunal has, however, to award compensation for expenses, pecuniary loss and also for pain and suffering. It can take notice of victim's behaviour and his contribution in commission of crime.

The foregoing study reveals that a new impetus started with human rights realisation at the world level. Victim oriented approach to criminal justice system became imperative and during last four to five decades there has been a move in right direction to provide restitution, compensation and assistance to the victims of crime. The lead of United Nations and U.S.A. is quite appreciative. But most of the countries of the world have come forward to follow the suit. Some countries have preferred the idea of restitutional justice and require offender to make amends to the losses suffered by the victim; some countries have regarded the State responsibility of providing compensation as a part of social security measure or welfare scheme on failure on the part of the State to provide security to its citizens. Assistance schemes have also been applied to cover a vide range of victims of domestic violence, atrocities, etc.

Notes and References

1. Webster, *New Dictionary of Synonyms*, G.U.C. Merrian, Springfield Mass (1968).
2. *The Oxford English Dictionary*, Clarendon Press (1933).
3. Das, Bharat B., *Victim in Criminal Justice System* (1997) A.P.H. Publishing Corporation, New Delhi, p. 26.
4. *Ibid.*
5. Council of Europe, Collections of Recommendations, Resolutions and Declaration of Ministers Concerning Human Rights, 1947-87, pp. 134-35 (1989), quoted from Bharat B. Das, Victims in Criminal Justice System (1997), p. 137.
6. Merryman, John Henry, *The Civil Law Tradition*, Stanford Univ. Press (1969), pp. 132-39.
7. Fletcher, Lawrence P. 'Restitution in Criminal Process: Procedure for Fixing the Offender's Liability *The Yale Law Journal* (1984), p. 505.
8. *Ibid.*, p. 266.
9. Das, B. Bharat, Victims in the Criminal Justice System (1997), p. 141.
10. Section 35(1), Criminal Court Act, 1973.
11. Section 35(A), Power of Criminal Court Act, 1973.
12. 60 Cr. APP. R. 70 (1974).
13. R.V. Thomson Holiday (1974) Q.B. 592 (Lawton L.J.).
14. R.V. Maynard 1983 Crim. L.R. 821.
15. Section 35(4) of Criminal Court Act, 1973.
16. Easton, Sushan and Piper, Christine, *Sentencing and Punishment* (The Quest for Justice) Oxford Univ. Press, pp. 180-81.
17. Zender, Lucia, *Victims*—The Oxford Handbook of Criminology, 3rd ed. Oxford Univ. Press, p. 441.
18. *Supra* n. 9, pp. 180-82.
19. Howard, C., "Compensation in French Criminal Procedure", *Modern Law Review*, 21 (1958), p. 387.
20. Horton, K.C., 'Criminal Injuries Compensation in West Germany', *New Law Journal*, 1980, p. 468.
21. Das, Bharat, B., *Victims in the Criminal Justice System* (1997), p. 154.
22. *Ibid.*

23. *Ibid.*
24. *Ibid.*, p. 156.
25. Law No. 990 of December 24, 1969.
26. Section 414 of the Penal Code of Norway.
27. Das, Bharat, B., Victims in the Criminal Justice System (1997), p. 160.
28. Camechon, Bruce J., "Compensation for Victims of Crime: Newzealand Experiment", *Journal of Public Law*, Vol. 12 (1963), pp. 367-75.

5

Restitutive Compensatory and Assistance Justice to the Victims of Crime under Statutory Provisions in India

The study in the earlier chapters have revealed the ever expanding definition of 'Victim', changing paradism of providing justice to the sufferers of loss due to wrongful acts of the offenders and expanding ways and means to put victim in right perspective so as to feel himself as an important segment of society and no more a 'forgotten man'. Many a provisions dealt under statutory provisions may not belong exactly to the criminal law[1] or even belonging to criminal law may not fit exactly into compensatory scheme[2] yet in view of the present day scenario and world wide developments they have been discussed in our study. It is so because at present the dividing line between the liability under criminal law and liability under tort is becoming very thin and purpose of doing justice with victims is getting prominence over technicality of the procedure followed.

I. COMPENSATORY JUSTICE TO VICTIMS UNDER Cr.P.C.

The Criminal procedure Code, 1973 provides for composition (compounding) and restitution as ways of compensation to the victims of crime. It envisages victims in wider sense of the term. Thus, it includes a person accused of defamation who was made so without reasonable cause and is acquitted,[3] accused without reasonable cause;[4] victim of a crime when case is disposed under provisions relating to plea bargaining;[5] person arrested groundlessly,[6] complainant of a non-cognizable offence incurring cost in the prosecution.[7] Section 357 is the main provision relating to compensation to the victims of crime.

An Abortive Attempt to Make Compensation as Substantive Punishment under I.P.C.

In historical perspective it is found that Criminal Procedure Code of 1898 provided for compensation to the victims of crime. But such provision contained in section 545 of the code could not be utilized well by the courts. It was realized that there should be substantive provision for payment of compensation to the victim of crime. The Law Commission of India in its 42nd Report recommended the amendment of the Indian Penal Code itself by incorporating compensation as a mode of punishment. Chapter III, para 19 of the Report read:

> "We think, however, that the Penal Code should give prominence to this aspect of compensating the victims of the offence out of the fine imposed on the offender. At present the legal provision in this regard is tucked away in the last miscellaneous chapter of the Code of Criminal Procedure. It seems to us that, as substantive power of the trial court, it deserves to be mentioned specifically in the Penal Code chapter on punishments along with the provisions relating to fines."[8]

Accepting the Report of the Law Commission of India Indian Penal Code Amendment Bill, 1972 was introduced in Rajya Sabha suggesting the amendment of section 53 of the

Indian Penal Code including *'order for payment of compensation'* as one of the modes of punishment. The Amendment Bill, 1972 stated in Notes on Clauses that:

> "The new provision is intended to provide for some kind of reparation of compensation to victims of crimes the need for which has been receiving attention in recent times. The existing provisions in section 545 of the Code of Criminal Procedure, 1898 are limited in scope and so a general power is being conferred on the convicting court to pass an order directing that the accused shall make compensation, restitution to any person aggrieved or injured or for the actual loss or damage arising from the commission of the offence, in such manner and to such extent as may be appropriate to the cases. The actual relief may take any form depending on the facts of the particular case and the court is expected to determine this question in a summary way without any elaborate inquiry. The direction for the compensation, restitution or reparation may be in addition to or in lieu of any other sentence, which the court may pass for the offence. It is considered that a provision of this bill be particularly beneficial to the poor section of the people where the accused is in a position to make amends."

The Law Commission of India in its 42nd Report had also suggested the payment of compensation to the victim of an offence out of fine imposed on the offender. It suggested insertion of Section 62 in the Indian Penal Code, 1860. The proposed section read:[9]

> *"Section 62. Order to pay compensation out of fine to victim of offence:* Whenever a person is convicted of an offence punishable under chapter 16 (which deals with offences affecting the human body) or chapter 17 (offences against property) or chapter 21 (dealing with offence of defamation) of this code or a abatement of such offence of a criminal conspiracy to commit such offence and is sentenced to a fine, whether with or without

imprisonment and the court is of opinion that compensation is recoverable by civil suit by any person for loss or injury caused to him by that offence, it shall be competent to the court to direct by the sentence that the whole or any part of the fine realized from the offender shall be paid by way of compensation to such person for the said loss or injury."

Explanation: Expenses properly incurred by such person in the prosecution of the case shall be deemed part of the loss caused to him by the offence.[10]

The attempt of the Law Commission to allow restitution/compensation as a sentencing option got aborted and could not find place in I.P.C through amendment Act. But restitution got place in section 357 of Cr.P.C. 1973. Under section 357 of Cr.P.C. (as it stands to day) the expression 'compensation' has been used in the sense of restitution.

As has been pointed out earlier some writers and learned Professors think that in technical sense compensatory or restitutional justice to the victims of crime has been incorporated only in section 357 of Cr.P.C. But in view the extended scope of victimology and wide meaning given to the expression 'victim', some other sections of Cr.P.C. 1973 are also discussed, so as to give a wider concern of victim-oriented justice.

(A) Compensatory Justice in Provisions other than Section 357 of Cr.P.C.

(i) Justice to Victim by Way of Composition or Compounding

Section 320, Cr.P.C. 1973 provides for composition as a way of doing Justice to the victims of the crimes. It encourages participation of both the victim and the offender and thereby has the healing impact with rehabilitative note. Section 320(1) gives a long table comprising of as many as 21 sections containing different types of crimes including wounding of religious feelings, hurt, restraint or confinement, assault or criminal use of force, criminal trespass, criminal breach of contract of service, adultery, enticement, defamation, insult, criminal intimidation, etc. The persons affected by such offences can compound or have compromise with the offender. Section 320(2) contains a table of 36 offences.[11] The person affected by such crime may compound or have compromise with the offender with permission of the Court before which any prosecution for such offence is pending. Section 320 provides for—

1. Offences compoundable between the victim/ affected party and the offender on their own with free compromise.
2. It provides for offences compoundable between the victim and the offender with permission of the Court. Such offences are more serious than the offences enumerated under the first category.
3. Abetment of compoundable offences constituting an offence is also compoundable.
4. If a person is otherwise competent to compound but suffers some infirmities for having become party of contract like the person being under age of eighteen years or being an idiot or a lunatic, any person competent to contract on his behalf may, with the permission of the court, compound such offence.

   In case of a victim or person otherwise competent to compound is dead his legal representative may compound such offence with permission of the court.
5. When the accused has been committed for trial or when he has been convicted and an appeal is pending, the composition can be allowed only with the leave of the Court to which he is committed, or, as the case may be before which the appeal is to be heard.
6. A compound of any offence may also be allowed to competent person to compound by the High Court or Court of session in exercise of its powers of revision under section 401.
7. The effect of the compound of offence shall be the acquittal of the accused with whom the offence has been compounded.

However, Section 320 does not allow compound of any offence in two situations. *First,* where accused is, by reason of a previous conviction, liable to enhanced punishment or to a punishment of a different kind for such offence, and *Second,* no offence shall be compounded except as provided under section 320. Speaking of this limitation in *Surendra Nath Mohanty* v. *State of Orissa*[12] the Supreme Court of India made clear that in view of the legislative mandate contained in section 320, Cr.P.C. only offences which are covered by Table 1 or 2 can be compounded and rest of the offences punishable under the Indian Penal Code cannot be compounded.

Section 320 of the present code is similar to Section 345 of the Criminal Procedure Code of 1898. The effect of compound is the acquittal of the offender. In *Kumaraswami Chetty* v. *Kuppuswami*[13] the Court ruled that once the composition is arrived at it has the effect of an acquittal so as to bar the trial of an offence. The calcutta High Court has expressed the view that a Magistrate cannot refuse to accept a compromise presented to him while he is writing his judgment.[14]

The main object of composition as a way of justice is to reinforce peace and amicable relations between the parties. Some times the Court takes practical view of the situation in allowing compromise. Thus, in *Saraswati Sutradhar* v. *State of Tripura*[15] a complaint was filed by wife against the husband. After elapse of time a prayer was made for compromise. The court found that husband and wife and their minor daughter were living peacefully for last two years without any disharmony among them. The High Court accepted the prayer of compromise but allowed composition with the reservation that instead of recording acquittal the operation of the impugned judgment of conviction and sentence be suspended for two years as a check on the possible deterioration of relationship between the husband and wife.

The role of superior courts in compound cases has been very practical. Sub-section (6) of section 320 empowers revision courts to allow a case to be compounded. An earlier decision of Calcutta High Court is very pertinent in this regard. In *Aminulla* v. *Emperror*[16] a bench of Calcutta High

Court observed:

> "It is a great pity when parties who are apparently nearly related to one another succeed-is patching up their quarrels that the Magistrate should not do what he can to restore peace and goodwill."

The Courts have generally insisted upon that no composition can be allowed in non-compoundable cases. But in certain exceptional cases with a view to achieve the end of justice superior courts have allowed composition as exceptional case with caution as to not to be treated as precedent. In *State* v. *Mohd. Akbar*[17] the appellants-respondents had been acquitted by the trial court due to compromise. The reason assigned for compounding the offence was that the complainant was bed-ridden and in her advance age wanted to die with a sense that she had no ill-will or grouse against the applicants-respondents. The Jammu and Kashmir High Court expressed the view that on facts and circumstances of the case relief claimed could be moulded to do justice between the parties. But it warned that the stand taken could not be cited as precedent that in each and every non-compoundable offence such a permission could be obtained as a matter of right. Such stand could be taken only in view of special circumstances.[18]

Similar stand was taken by the Apex Court in *Y. Suresh Babu* v. *State of A.P.*[19] The facts of the case were as such: The appellant had been convicted under section 326 of the Indian Penal Code, 1860 and sentenced to under go rigorous imprisonment for a period of one year. Although the offence under Section 326 of the Code is non-compoundable, learned counsel for the parties submitted that through the intervention of well-wishers the parties who belonged to the same locality had reconciled their differences to preserve amity and good relations. They prayed for leave to compound the offence. It was noted that the appellant had stabbed D. Narsinga Rao, Respondent No. 2 after an altercation near the pan shop owned by him. The counsel for appellant submitted that it was an unfortunate incident and his client had a feeling of remorse. The counsel appearing for respondent No. 2 also joined in the prayer for permission to compound the offence. Keeping in view the overall facts and circumstances of the case of Division Bench of the Supreme Court of India consisting Mr. Justice A.P. Sen and Mr. Justice B.C. Ray granted leave as a special case to the parties to compound the offence on condition that appellant paid Rs. 10,000 to Respondent 2 by way of compensation for the physical injury suffered by him. The Court, however, directed that it should not be treated as a precedent.

In allowing composition in exceptional cases the Supreme Court has been guided by the well-being of both the parties. In *Narottam Singh* v. *State of Punjab,*[20] the Supreme Court allowed a compromise through compounding in a case under section 494 (compoundable with permission of Court). The compounding was allowed on payment of Rs. 40,000 to the victim-wife and on payment of Rs. 4,000 as costs. The Supreme Court remarked that "the compensation for his sexual aberration and breaking up of the matrimonial home will instill a correctional responsibility on the man." It also noted that acquittal following upon the composition, will hopefully save his business, and avert the hurtful jail term. The consent to divorce by the complainant will put as under in law the marital tie which in fact has long ago sundered.[21]

Some High Courts have allowed compounding of cases under section 498-A of the Indian Penal Code, though it is not enumerated either under the table of clause (1) or clause (2) of section 320 of Cr.P.C., 1973. Thus, in *State* v. *Gopilal*[22] the compounding of offence under section 498-A of the Indian Penal Code was allowed where a wife condoned the cruelty of her husband. It was done so even though in a separate civil petition for restitution of conjugal rights by the husband against his wife allegation of cruelty was not proved. In *Gurusharan Kaur* v. *State of Rajasthan*[23] on information of Gurusharan Kaur case was registered against her husband Baldev Singh and father-in-law under section 408 and section 498-A. The parties had compounded their dispute and were living together. In facts and circumstances of the case the petition was allowed as it was thought that it was in the interest of the parties that the said offences were compounded.

It is submitted in view of the provision of sub-section (9) of section 320 which reads, "No offence shall be compounded except as provided by this sections", non-compoundable offences, that is to say which are not included in Tables attached to clauses (1) and (2) of section 320, cannot be compounded. As Karnataka High Court pointed out in *State of Karnataka* v. *H.S. Srinivas Iyengar*[24] that in view of clear position of law (i.e. section 320(9) Cr.P.C.) the non-compoundable offences cannot be compounded even in exercise of inherent power of the High Court under section 482 of the Code of Criminal Procedure, 1973. The same view has been shared by the Full Bench of Andhra Pradesh High Court in *Ghousia Sultana* v. *Mohd. Ghouse Baig.*[25] The Supreme Court decision in *Bankat and Another* v. *State of Mahrastra*[26] reaffirms that in view of sub-section (2) of section 320 of Cr.P.C. 1973 and the legislative mandate given in it only offences which are covered by Table 1 or Table 2 can be compounded and rest of the offences punishable under I.P.C. cannot be compounded.

A perusal of case law on the point presents two opinions:

1. In certain exceptional circumstances non-compoundable offence may be compounded. This view finds support due to the decisions of the Supreme Court in *Ram Pujan Patel* v. *State of U.P.*[27], *Y. Suresh Babu* v. *State of U.P.*[28] and *Mahesh Chand* v. *State of U.P.*[29]
2. In view of section 320(9) non-compoundable offences cannot be compounded in any case. This view is settled in *Ram Lal* v. *State of J. and K.*[30], *Bankat* v. *State of Maharashtra,*[31] *Surendra Nath Mohanthy* v. *State of Orissa.*[32]

The final judicial verdict is in favour of treating or allowing non-compoundable offendes as compoundable in no case. The Supreme Court referred to *Ram Pujan Patel's case*[33] in *Bankat* v. *State of Maharastra*[34] and held that it did not support the case of making non-compoundable cases compoundable. In latter case *Ram Lal's case*[35] was approvingly cited wherein the Supreme Court disagreed with *Y. Suresh Babu's* case[36] and and *Mahesh Chand's case*[37] and observed.

> "We are unable to follow the said decision (Mahesh Chand's) as a binding precedent. Section 320 which deals with 'compounding of offences' provides two tables therein, one containing descriptions of offences which can be compounded by the person mentioned in it, and the other containing descriptions of offences which can be compounded with the permission of the Court by the person indicated therein. Only such offences as are included in the said two Tables can be compounded and none else."

Thus, the cases allowing non-compoundable offences as compoundable in certain exceptional circumstances have been declared as having no binding effect. They can be treated as per incuriam as pointed attention of the Court to sub-section (9) of Section 320 was not drawn. The cases allowing non-compoundable offences as compoundable have been declared not to be in accordance with law.

It is submitted with due regard that the Supreme Court decisions may be appreciable in view of positivistic jurisprudential approach, i.e. treating law as it is. Such decisions may be appreciated in framework of the literal interpretation. But in view of Section 482 of Cr.P.C.[38], 1973 and Article 142 of the Constitution of India[39], the High Courts and the Supreme Court of India should have been conceded the activist role to meet the end of Justice. No wonder the composition or settlement of disputes by the parties outside the court has been given due credence even in those cases where the non-compoundable offences have not been allowed to be compounded. The remedy is shifted from Section 320 to Section 357. Thus, in *Bankat* v. *State of Maharastra*[40] itself the Supreme Court observed:

> "However, considering the fact that the parties have settled their dispute outside the court, the fact that 10 years have elapsed from the date of the incident and the further fact that the appellants have already

undergone several imprisonments, ends of justice would be met if the sentence of imprisonment is reduced to a period already undergone besides imposing a fine of Rs. 5000 on each of the accused under Section 326 read with section 34 IPC. Out of the fine amount if realised, a sum of Rs. 4000 also be paid to each of the injured as compensation."

(ii) Compensation to Persons Groundlessly Arrested

Section 358, Cr.P.C. 1973 provides for doing justice with a person who is arrested groundlessly and thereby becomes victim. Section 358(1) reads:

> "Whenever any person causes a police officer to arrest another person, if it appears to the Magistrate by whom the case is heard that there was no sufficient ground for causing such arrest, the Magistrate may award such compensation, not exceeding one hundred rupees, to be paid by the person so causing the arrest to the person so arrested, for his loss of time and expenses in the matter, as the Magistrate thinks fit."

Section 358(2) provides for compensation to more than one persons if more persons are arrested groundlessly. Section 358(3) makes the amount of compensation recoverable as if it were fine. In the case of failure of recovery the person by whom compensation is payable shall be sentenced to simple imprisonment for such term not exceeding thirty days as the Magistrate directs. In *Shah Chandulal Gokaldas Patel* v. *Baldev bhai Ranchhoddas*[41] the Gujarat High Court pointed out that while making order to pay compensation by person causing the groundless arrest of another person the Magistrate must follow the principle of natural justice. He should give an opportunity of showing cause and trying to satisfy the Magistrate that there was sufficient ground for causing arrest. If complainant or the person who caused the alleged wrongful arrest fails to satisfy the Magistrate, then only Magistrate should order the payment of compensation. In *Mallappa* v. *Veerabasappa*,[42] it was pointed out that some direct and proximate, nexus between the complaint and arrest is contemplated for applying Section 358, Cr.P.C. the test should be that but for the efforts of the complainant, the arrest could not have been affected.

(iii) Compensation for Accusation without Reasonable Cause

Section 250, Cr.P.C., 1973 provides for compensation for accusation without reasonable cause. Section 250(1) reads: If, in any case instituted upon complaint or upon information given to a police officer or to a Magistrate, one or more persons is or are accused before a Magistrate of any offence triable by a Magistrate, and the Magistrate by whom the case is heard discharges or acquits all or any of the accused, and is of opinion that there was no reasonable ground for making the accusation against them or any of them, the Magistrate may, by his order of discharge or acquittal, if the person upon whose complaint or information accusation was made is present, call upon him forthwith to show cause why he should be not pay compensation to such accused or to each or any of such accused when there are more than one; or if such person is not present, direct the issue of a summons to him to appear and show cause as aforesaid.

Thus, the Magistrate might have discharged or acquitted the accused. He must be of opinion that there was no reasonable ground for accusation. He must issue show cause notice to the person on whose complaint or information is accusation was made.[43]

In such circumstances of satisfaction of the Magistrate and having issued show cause notice, the Magistrate has to satisfy himself that there was no reasonable ground for making of accusation, thereafter Magistrate has to record reasons and then make an order of compensation be paid by such complainant or informant to the accused or to each or any of them.[44] In default of payment of compensation a term of simple imprisonment for a period not exceeding one month can also be ordered by the Magistrate. During imprisonment the person so imprisoned will be released on payment of the amount of compensation or proportional part of compensation.[45] However, the order of compensation under section 250 of Cr.P.C. does not exempt such person from any civil or criminal liability in respect of the complaint made or information given by him.[46] But any amount paid to an accused person under section 250 shall be taken into account in awarding compensation to such person in any subsequent civil suit relating to the same matter.[47] An order of compensation exceeding one hundred rupees is appealable as if such complainant or informant had been convicted on a trial held by such Magistrate.[48] Compensation shall not be paid before the period allowed for the presentation of the appeal has elapsed, or if appeal is presented, before the appeal has been decided and in case of non-appealable matter one month from the date of order.[49] The provisions of Section 350 apply to both Summons cases and Warrant cases.[50]

The compensation order under Section 250 has to be made with great caution. Its purpose is to discourage false accusation preferred recklessly or maliciously. It should not have had effect of discouraging legitimate grievance redressal.[51] Discharge or acquittal of the accused is condition precedent for order of compensation.[52] As pointed out by Madras High Court the principle of giving compensation is recompense by way of damages to the party who has been vexatiously dragged before a Criminal Court.[53]

Section 250, (old being the same) allows compensation only to the person who has suffered by the offence and not to the suffer's relations.[54] However, the compensation is awardable to the survivors who suffered loss of a pecuniary nature.[55]

The amount of compensation must not exceed the maximum fixed by the section. But it may exceed if there are number of accused persons. The Magistrate while assessing compensation may be guided by the loss sustained or the inconvenience undergone by the accused.

(iv) Justice to Victim through payment of Costs in non-cognizable offences

Section 359(1) provides "whenever any complaint of a non-cognizable offence is made to a Court, the Court, if it convicts the accused, may, in addition to the penalty imposed upon him, order him to pay, to the complainant, in whole or in part, the cost incurred by him in the prosecution, and may further order that in default of payment, the accused shall suffer simple imprisonment for a period not exceeding thirty days and such costs may include any expenses incurred in respect of process-fees, witnesses and pleader's fees which the Court may consider reasonable."

The Appellate Court or the High Court or Court of Session may also order as to payment of costs. Costs may include Advocate's fees.

(v) Compensation in case of plea Bargaining

Act No. 2 of 2006 inserted Chapter XXI-A in Cr.P.C., 1973. It introduced the idea of plea bargaining.

The concept of plea bargaining and its recognition in the form of statutory provision has very interesting history. It is very popular in the United States. In India it could not get approval of the apex Court. The apex court had disapproved it in *State of U.P.* v. *Chandrika.*[56] The Allahabad High Court had accepted the plea bargaining and maintained the conviction of the respondent under Section 304 Part I of the Indian Penal Code but altered the sentence to the period of imprisonment already undergone by the respondent accused plus a fine of Rs. 5,000. The single judge of Allahabad High Court (Malvia, J.) had done so after accepting the bargain initiated by the accused. The Division Bench of the Supreme Court consisting of K.T. Thomas and M.B. Shah, JJ. declared the order passed by the High Court as illegal and erroneous on the face of it. Speaking through Shah, J. the Supreme Court pointed out that the concept of plea bargaining is not recognized and is against public policy under our criminal justice system. The Court ruled that such a practice cannot be encouraged except compounding of certain offences under section 320 of the Code of Criminal Procedure. The apex court categorically ruled out disposal of the criminal cases on the basis of "plea bargaining." It was asserted that "mere acceptance or admission of the guilt should not be a ground for reduction of sentence. Nor can the accused bargain with the Court that he is pleading guilty the sentence be reduced." The Court was more apprehensive of its misuse in cases of dangerous economic offences and food crimes.

The statutory recognition of "plea bargaining" has been

given despite the above decision of the Supreme Court. But the apprehension of misuse has been appreciated by providing exception in three categories of cases (discussed later) including statutes affecting socio-economic conditions of the country. Thus, it is submitted that the legislative measure of plea bargaining presents a compromise between the emerging necessity of allowing plea bargaining as a way of doing justice to both the victim and the offender and keeping certain offences outside its purview.[57]

Section 265 E(a) deals with compensation in the case of plea bargaining. It reads: "the court shall award the compensation to the victim in accordance with the disposition under Section 265D . . ."

Sections 265A to 265L have been incorporated in newly inserted Chapter XXI-A. Award of compensation under plea bargaining is allowed under certain circumstances and with certain conditions—

1. The report has been forwarded by the office-in-charge of the Police Station under Section 173 alleging therein that an offence appears to have been committed by him.
2. But the offence is not of very serious nature, i.e. (i) it is offence other than an offence for the which the punishment of death, or (ii) of imprisonment for life or imprisonment for a term exceeding seven years has been provided under the law for time being in force.
3. A Magistrate has taken cognizance of the above nature of the offence and after examining complainant and witnesses under Section 200 has issued the process under Section 204.
4. A person accused of an offence will file an application for plea bargaining in the Court in which such offence is pending for trial.

   The application will narrate circumtances of the offence and with affidavit swear that the application is made voluntarily after understanding the nature and extent of punishment provided under the law for offence. It should also state that the offender has not previously been convicted by a court in a case in which he had been charged with the same offence.

5. The Court after receiving the plea bargaining application shall issue notice to Public Prosecutor or the complainant, as the case may be, and to the accused to appear on the date fixed for the case.
6. When Public Prosecutor or Complainant, as the case may be, and the accused appear on the date fixed, the Court shall examine accused in camera where other party shall not be present. The Court will do so with a view to satisfy that the accused has filed the application voluntarily. When the Court is satisfied to this effect it shall provide time to public prosecutor or the complainant, as the case may be and the accused to work out mutually satisfactory disposition of the case which may include giving to the victim by the accused compensation and other expenses during the case and thereafter fix date for next hearing. On the date of next hearing Public Prosecutor, Police Officer who had investigated the case, the accused and the victim shall participate in meeting to workout a satisfactory disposition of the case. The Court shall ensure that entire process is completed voluntarily. The accused, if desires will be allowed to appear with his pleader.
7. If the case is instituted otherwise than on police report, the Court will call both victim and accused, ensure voluntarily disposition and allow participation with pleader, if the accused or victim so desire.
8. Where in the meeting a satisfactory disposition of the case has been worked out, the Court shall prepare a report of such disposition which shall be signed by the presiding officer of the Court and all other persons who participated in the meeting.

Accordingly the Court shall award compensation to the victim as per disposition and hear the parties on the quantum of the punishment, releasing of the accused on probation of good conduct or after admonition under Section 360 or dealing with the accused under the provisions of the Probation of Offendender Act, 1958 or any other law for the time being enforce.[58]

Compensation by way of plea bargaining is positive step taken by the accused himself and therefore may satisfy victim with healing touch. However, it is not always appreciated. The former Judge of the Supreme Court of India K.T. Thomas (who had been party to the earlier referred decision in his recent article contributed in *Hindu* Open Page Column) has spoken of plea-bargain as a fillip to Criminal Courts and regards the advantages which include speedy disposal of cases, outweigh its demerits. Though it presents innovation in our criminal justice system, but there are certain demerits also. *Firstly,* the plea bargaining process reduces the administration of criminal justice to a barter system, where haggling is between legal punishment and gains to the wrong doer. *Secondly,* even innocent accused may be tempted to adopt the procedure with a view to escape from ordeal of a prolonged and expensive trial. *Thirdly,* the cases in which accused might finally secured acquittal would be converted into cases of unmerited conviction. *Finally,* it may amount to violation of Article 21 of the Constitution.

There are certain categories of cases which have been excluded from the scope of plea bargaining. They include: (i) offences affecting socio-economic conditions of the country; (ii) offences committed against women; and (iii) offences committed against children below the age of 14 years.

It is submitted that despite its limitations and certain demerits, the advantages of plea bargaining would outweigh its shortcomings and will smoothen the relation between the offender and the victim and thereby will be helpful in peaceful co-existence in society.

(B) Compensatory/Restitutive Justice to the Victims of Crime under Section 357, Cr.P.C., 1973

For long there has been and to some extent still is accusation that the criminal justice system thinks more of the rights of the offender than that of relief to the victims. Section

357 of the Code of Criminal Procedure, 1973 presents some consolation to victim oriented criminal justice jurists. Its object is to provide compensation to the persons who are entitled to recover damages from person sentenced even though fine does not form part of the sentence.

Section 357, Cr.P.C., 1973 is the main statutorily recognized restitutive provision aiming at doing justice with the victims of crime. It has been sufficiently improved upon earlier section 545 of the old code. Clauses (3) and (4) have been newly added to fulfil the emerging requirement of criminal justice leaving victim no more a 'forgotten man' but accepting him as a social man having vital role to play in society.

Section 357(1) reads:

> "(1) When a court imposes a sentence of fine or a sentence (including a sentence of death) of which fine forms a part, the court may, when passing Judgment, order the whole or any part of the fine recovered to be applied—
>
> (a) in defraying the expenses properly incurred in the prosecution;
>
> (b) in the payment of any person of compensation for any loss or injury caused by the offence, when compensation is, in opinion of the court, recoverable by such person in a civil court;
>
> (c) when any person is convicted of any offence for having caused the death of another person or of having abetted the Commission of such an offence, in paying compensation to the persons who are, under the Fatal Accidents Act, 1855 (13 of 1855), entitled to recover damages from the person sentenced for the loss of resulting to them from such death;
>
> (d) when any person is convicted of any offence which includes theft, criminal misappropriation, criminal breach of trust, or cheating, or having dishonestly received or retained, or having voluntarily assisted in disposing of stolen property knowingly or having reason to

> believe the same to be stolen, in compensating any *bona fide* purchaser of such property for the loss of the same if such property is restored to the possession of the person entitled thereto."[59]

However, if the fine is imposed in a case which is subject to appeal, no such payment shall be made before the period allowed for presenting the appeal has elapsed, or if an appeal be presented, before the decision of the appeal.

Sub-section (3) of Section 357 empowers the Court to order compensation in cases wherein fine does not form a part. It reads: "when a court imposes a sentence, of which fine does not forma part, the court may, when passing judgment order the accused person to pay, by way of compensation such amount as may be specified in the order to the person who has suffered any loss or injury by reason of the act for which the accused person has been so sentenced.

An Appellate Court or the High Court or the Court of Session may also made order of compensation under Section 357 when exercising the power of revision.

However, there is scope for adjustment when the matter is taken up in a subsequent civil suit. Thus, at the time of awarding compensation in any subsequent civil suit relating to the same matter, the Court shall take into account any sum paid or recovered as compensation under section 357.

A number of states like Andhra Pradesh, Bihar, Karnataka, Madhya Pradesh, Rajasthan, U.P. and West Bengal have made certain amendments while applying the principle of compensation in relation to the Scheduled Castes and Scheduled Tribes.

For Uttar Pradesh Section 357 reads thus:

(a) In Sub-section (1) after Clause (d), the following Proviso shall be Inserted, namely:

> "Provided that if a person who may receive compensation under Clauses (b), (c) and (d) is a member of the Scheduled Castes or the Scheduled

Tribes and the person sentenced is not a member of such castes or Tribes, the Court shall order the whole or any part of the fine recovered to be applied in the payment of such compensation."

(b) For Sub-section (3) the following Sub-section shall be Substituted, namely:

"(3) When a Court imposes a sentence, of which fine, does not form a part, the Court may, and where the person who has suffered the loss or injury is a member of the Scheduled Castes or the Scheduled Tribes and the person sentenced is not a member of such Castes or Tribes, the Court shall, when passing judgment, order the person sentenced to pay, by way of compensation, such amount as may be specified in the order to the person who has suffered any loss or injury by reason of the act for which the person has been so sentenced."

Section 357 is improvement upon earlier section 545 of the Code of Criminal Procedure, 1898. Earlier provision had limited the order of compensation to cases where substantial compensation was recoverable by the injured party. While commenting upon the use of expression 'substantial' in Section 545(1)(b) of the old code, the Law Commission had expressed the view that—

"The significance of the requirement compensation should be recoverable in a civil court is that the act which constitutes the offence in question should also be a tort. The word "substantial" appears to have been used to exclude cases where only nominal damages would be recoverable. We think it hardly necessary to emphasize this aspect since in any event it is purely within the discretion of the criminal courts to order or not to order payment of compensation, and in practice they are not particularly liberal in insisting on this provision."

The Law Commission suggested the deletion of the

word *substantial* and made clear that "under the new provision, compensation can be awarded irrespective of whether the offence is punishable with fine and fine is actually imposed, but such compensation can be ordered only if the accused is convicted. The compensation should be payable for any loss or injury whether physical or pecuniary, and the court shall have due regard to the nature of injury, the manner of inflicting the same, the capacity of the accused to pay and other relevant factors."[60]

The new Section 357 has not used the expression 'substantial' therefore, the court is free to award compensation irrespective of the fact whether fine is substantially recoverable by the person at civil court or not. Section 357 makes specific provisions for awarding compensation in two types of cases—

(i) award of compensation out of fine that is imposed under the law, and

(ii) award of compensation where a Court imposes sentence of which fine does not form a part.

The power of the Court to order compensation is not ancillary to the other sentences but it is in addition thereto. It is intended to do something to reassure the victim that he or she is not forgotten in the criminal justice system. Five trends are discernible in relation to award of compensation under Section 357 of the Code of Criminal Procedure, 1973.

(i) By and Large the Power to Order Compensation has not been Exercised Liberally

The Law Commission of India in its Forty-first Report noted that the provisions of Section 357 have not been particularly liberally utilized and lamented that, "it is regrettable that our Courts do not exercise their statutory powers under this section as freely and liberally as they could be desired." [61]

Though some of High Courts had appreciated the object of Section 357, Cr.P.C. 1973, but the approach of the highest Court of land during 1960s and 1970s was not very much encouraging. Thus, in *Surinder Singh* v. *The State*,[62] the

Full bench of Punjab and Haryana High Court pronounced a landmark decision in the history of the victim's right to compensation. The High Court observed that it is desirable that the trial Court in all appropriate cases, should consider the question of award of compensation at the time of passing the sentence. The social purpose intended to be served by Section 357 should be given due credence. On the other hand *Adamaji Umar* v. *State of Bombay*,[63] the Supreme Court observed that while passing a sentence the Court has always to bear in mind the necessity of proportion between an offence and the penalty. The Court has to look into the pecuniary circumstance of the accused person and to the magnitude of the sentence. Where a substantial term of imprisonment is imposed, an excessive fine could not be imposed except in exceptional cases. In *Planiapa Gounder* v. *State of Tamil Nadu*,[64] the victim oriented approach adopted by the High Court was not approved by the Supreme Court on technical legal grounds. The session Court convicted the appellant under Section 302 of the Indian Penal Code and sentenced him to death. On appeal the High Court upheld the appellants conviction under section 302 of the I.P.C. But it converted death penalty into imprisonment for life. While doing to the High Court imposed a fine of Rs. 20,000 on the appellant and directed that out of the fine a sum of Rs. 15,000 should be paid as compensation to the heirs of the deceased under Section 357(1)(c) of the Criminal Procedure Code. In fact the High Court's, good gesture was shown in view of an application filed by the heirs of the deceased before the High Court asking for compensation of Rs. 40,000 for the death of their father. The application was made under Section 482 of Cr.P.C. 1973 which invests in the High Court the inherent power to do justice. However, the High Court did not pass order under that provision. It passed order under Section 357(1)(c) of the Code of Criminal Procedure. The Supreme Court did not approve of the stand taken by the High Court. It elaborately came with heavy hands—

(1) The High Court order was not warranted by Section 482 Cr.P.C. 1973 because, "the provision which saves the inherent power of a court cannot

override any express provision contained in any statute which saves that power." In other words, in view of the express provision of Section 357 there was no scope for the High Court for invoking Section 482 exercising inherent power. The High Court had to apply the provisions of the Statute advisedly made to govern a particular subject-matter.

(2) The compensation order to be paid was higher than the compensation which had to come out of fine.

(3) The sentence including sentence of fine must be proportionate to the nature of offence.

(4) While awarding compensation out of fine the first thing to be considered is whether the fine is at all called for. Particularly it is more essential in cases of the sentence of death or life imprisonment.

The Supreme Court pointed out that excessive fine could not be awarded and reduced the fine of Rs. 20,000 imposed by the High Cort on the accused, who was sentenced to life imprisonment, to a sum of Rs. 3,000.

It is submitted that the Supreme Court did not lay down guide lines for awarding compensation. It also did not look into the provisions of Section 357(3) which allows order of compensation which does not form part of fine. The victim compensation law received a set back in the decision of the Supreme Court.

The judicial outlook to limit compensation to be paid to the victim of crime out of fine only does not represent a healthy trend. But the Supreme Court did not make any departure from its earlier stand and reiterated it in *Sarwan Singh* v. *State of Punjab*.[65] In this case five accused persons armed with various weapons caused injuries to the deceased which resulted in his death. The lower court ordered compensation to the dependants of the deceased for loss suffered by them. The High Court assessed the compensation of Rs. 20,000 on the basis that the deceased was aged about 48 years and was actively supervising the cultivation of the family land and could have lived another 15 to 20 years with his ability intact to supervise cultivation of family land. Thus the loss to the sons and daughters was calculated about 20,000. The Supreme Court in appeal pointed out that there was no warrant for the assumption made by the High Court as regards the retention of "ability intact" or as regards the extent of "loss to the dependants." The Supreme Court characterized what the High Court had done as "putting the Cart before the horse" in leaving the propriety to depend upon the amount of compensation. In this case too the opinion of the Supreme Court centred around the idea of award of compensation under section 357(1) even if fine was not a part of the sentence.

The observation of the Supreme Court in *Sarwan Singh* v. *State of Punjab*[66] is clear indication of the narrow outlook towards compensatory justice to the victim of crime. The Court ruled—

1. "The object of the section is to provide compensation payable to the persons who are entitled to recover damage from the person sentenced even though fine does not form part of the sentence.
2. In awarding compensation it is necessary for the Court to decide whether the case is fit one in which compensation has to be awarded.
3. If it is found that compensation should be paid, then the capacity of the accused to pay compensation has to be determined.
4. In directing compensation the object is to collect the fine and pay it to the person who has suffered the loss. The purpose will not be served, if the accused is not able to pay the fine or compensation, for imposition of a default sentence for non-payment of fine would not achieve the object.
5. It is the duty of the Court to take into account the nature of the claim for compensation, the capacity of the accused to pay and other relevant circumstances in fixing the amount of fine or compensation."

The trend shown by the Supreme Court was again followed in *Brij Lal* v. *Prem Chand*[67] and *State of Uttar Pradesh* v. *Jodh Singh*.[68] In *Brij Lal* v. *Prem Chand*[69] the deceased Veena who died of burn injuries was married to the respondent Prem Chand, the accused. Prem Chand used to demand money from deceased wife and use quarrel every day over payment of money. On fateful date the deceased reacted by saying that she preferred death to life in this world. Accused added fuel to five by saying that she could provide him relief quicker by dying over the same day. Deceased set fire on herself immediately thereafter. The fact that the accused had demanded Rs. 10,000 on fateful date from the wife, had quarrel and instigated her to commit suicide was enough to prove his crime under Section 306 of I.P.C. The trial Court convicted him but the High Court acquitted the accused. On appeal the Supreme Court set aside the decision of the High Court and restored the conviction by the trial Court. Keeping view that accused had undergone 10 months imprisonment and eleven years had elapsed since the High Court had acquitted him and was leading a settled life, the Supreme Court substituted sentence awarded to accused with sentence of imprisonment for period already undergone by him and enhanced the sentence of fine from Rs. 500 to Rs. 20,000. The Supreme Court also directed that out of the fine amount, if paid, a sum of Rs. 18,000 should be paid to the father of deceased for bringing up deceased's minor son. The compensation was awarded out of fine, i.e. under Section 357(1) Cr.P.C. and Court appeared more sympathetic towards the accused rather than the victim.

In *State of Uttar Pradesh* v. *Jodh Singh*[70] in a quarrel accused party attacked deceased party. Two of the deceased party died of injuries and third person sustained several injuries. They were convicted under section 302 read with Section 147 and 148 I.P.C. and section 307 read with section 149 I.P.C. by the Session Judge. But on appeal the High Court set aside the conviction and acquitted all of them. On appeal Supreme Court acquitted two of the accused but convicted 5 (A-2 to A-6) under Section 304 Part II read with Section 341, I.P.C. On the question of sentence the Supreme Court took the view that since the occurrence had taken place nearly 17 years ago and since the accused were acquitted 11 years ago, the purpose of resending them to imprison would not be just in view of the fact that all accused had settled down to their normal avocation and were looking after their family members. The Court realised that by sending them to rest of the term of imprisonment would cause them as well as their family members very great hardship. Hence the Court sentenced them to the period of imprisonment already under gone by them. In addition sentenced A-2 to 4 and A-6 to pay a fine of Rs. 5000 (five thousand only) and A-5 to pay a fine of Rs. 2500 (Two thousand and five hundred). The Supreme Court directed 75% of fine amount to be given in equals to the two heirs of the deceased. The court also sentenced a fine of Rs. 250 under section 326/34 of the Indian Penal Code and directed that 75% of the amount be given to the P.W.I who was also victim as injured person.

The judicial trend to allow compensation under Section 357(1) out of the sentence of fine imposed on accused is not very much encouraging for the victim's right to get compensation. It is discretionary. If fine is imposed not at all, the victim cannot get compensation. Section 357(1) has its own limitations. *Firstly,* the award of compensation is co-terminus with the imposition of substantive sentence of fine. If substantive sentence of fine is not imposed, payment of compensation to the victim cannot be ordered; *Secondly,* compensation can be ordered only out of fine levied and not in addition to it. *Thirdly,* compensation order can serve fruitful purpose only if the fine is realized. If the fine is not realized, compensation order cannot materialize. *Fourthly,* the quantum of compensation could in no case exceed the amount of fine imposed and amount of fine will depend on nature of a particular offence and jurisdiction of the Court to impose fine. *Fifthly,* Courts have been reductant to impose maximum amount of fine prescribed by the Indian Penal Code. In addition Courts take into account the nature of crime, the injury suffered, capacity of the offender to pay, claim of victim, etc. *Lastly,* compensation is awarded to victim out of fine only when it is of the opinion that the compensation is recoverable by victim in a civil court. Thus, offence in question should also constitute a tort.

Thus, section 357(1) leaves many unanswered questions viz. what happens to claim of compensation to the victim if no fine is imposed? or when fine imposed is not realized or no case for damages in civil court is made out by the sentencing court? or, situation in which the accused is not convicted or let off on probation? or where accused is not in a position to pay the fine imposed?

(ii) Sentence is Reduced in Case of Increase or Fresh Imposition of the Amount of Fine

One tendency discernible in courts attitude is that were court increases the amount of fine under Section 357(1) it reduces the sentence imposed on the accused. In cases discussed earlier is *Brijlal* v. *Pre Chand*[71] and *State of U.P.* v. *Jodh Singh*,[72] we have observed that the Court reduced the sentence to period of imprisonment already undone and imposed fine. In *Nanda Ballabh Pant* v. *State*,[73] the accused was convicted under Section 304-A of the Indian Penal Code, i.e. causing death by negligence. He was sentenced to two months rigorous imprisonment and fine of Rs. 500. The Supreme Court reduced the sentence of imprisonment to one month and enhanced the amount of fine to Rs. 1000 and directed the same to be paid to the wife of the deceased by way of compensation.

In *Guruswamy* v. *State of Tamil Nadu*,[74] the accused convicted on charge of murder and was sentenced to death. On appeal the Supreme Court reduced the sentence to imprisonment for life and imposed a fine of Rs. 10,000. The Court directed to pay the amount of fine to the widow and her minor children as compensation for loss they had suffered by the death of the deceased. In other cases which are not like them indicating special consideration in view of offender enjoying longer period of acquittal by the High Court, the courts have reduced the period of imprisonment or nature of punishment and enhanced fine. In *Sarup Singh* v. *State of Haryana*[75] the accused was found guilty of an offence under Section 307, I.P.C. and was punished accordingly. He had been under custody for over one year and had also been under custody for some time during investigation of the case and trial. The Supreme Court reduced his sentence of imprisonment to a period already undergone. But a additional sentence of fine of Rs. 20,000 was imposed with direction to pay the widow of the deceased under the provision of Section 357 of the Code of Criminal Procedure, 1973. In *Balraj* v. *State of U.P.*,[76] the accused killed his elder brother, his four minor daughters, one son and one guest and attempted to kill his wife. He was sentenced to death. The Supreme Court of India noted that it was not a "rarest of rare" case as the accused at the time of committing the crime was under extreme mental and emotional disturbance apprehending his own death at the instance of the deceased. The Supreme Court awarded a compensation of Rs. 10,000 to the deceased's wife.

In *A. Babu Rao* v. *State of Andhra Pradesh*[77] the accused/appellant was charged with an offence punishable under section 376 of the Indian Penal Code. The crime was not compoundable. But an attempt was made by the victim girl and her elderly persons to arrive at a compromise. It could not materialize as accused-appellant was not able to pay Rs. 10,000 as demanded by the parents of the victim girl. The Andhra Pradesh High Court took the lenient view in the circumstances of the case and reduced the sentence and directed the accused to suffer rigorous imprisonment of two years. The fine of Rs. 5,000 imposed by the trial Court was enhanced to Rs. 10, 000 out of which Rs. 5,000 was directed to be paid to the victim girl.

(iii) Ends of Justice is Served if Compensation is Paid to Victim

In *Bhojappa Hanmanthappa Choudannavar* v. *State of Karnataka*[78] the Supreme Court allowed compensation to the victims' father in lieu of imprisonment of the offender with a view to meet the ends of Justice. The facts of the case were that a commotion took place in front of the House of Bhimappa during the night of 10.9.1984. The appellant and his co-accused were involved in assaulting Bhimappa and his brothers-in-law. While brawl was in full swing Bhimappa's daughter Renu Kavva, a twelve-year-old little girl, rushed to the scene. She did so presumably to rescue her father whom she would have thought to be in a dangerous situation. The appellant had a wooden hammer at that time in hand and hit by that Renu Kavva. That hit unfortunately turned out to be fatal. The first appellant and other accused were acquitted by the trial court. The High Court reversed the order of acquittal and convicted the first appellant accused under 304 part II and section 323 of the Indian Penal Code and sentenced him to rigorous imprisonment for three years on the first count and to a fine of Rs. 500 on the second count. On appeal the Supreme Court noted the death of a little girl as an unfortunate incident. But felt that appellant had no ire against that little girl before or during the occurrence. It was an act done in a rash mood without any intention to cause even grievous hurt to the girl. There was only one injury which the little girl sustained and probably because the skull bone of the deceased was not grown to sturdiness as in grown-up-persons the strike had resulted in such a calamitous proportion. The Court, however, realised that accused must pay penalty. The division Bench of K.T. Thomas and M.B. Shah, JJ. while confirming the conviction under Section 304 Part II of the I.P.C. altered the sentence to a fine of Rs. 25,000. The Court observed: "After considering various aspects we think that a fine of Rs. 25,000 is necessary to meet the end of Justice." The Court also directed that if the fine is realized from the appellant the same amount should be paid to Bhimappa (the father of Renu Kavva) by way of compensation under Section 357(1) of the Code of Criminal Procedure.

In *Joshi* v. *State of Kerala*,[79] the petitioner was prepared to pay a fine of Rs. one lakh. Taking into consideration the facts and circumstances of the case, the sentence of imprisonment of five years imposed upon the petitioner accused was modified in one of fine. In lieu of the sentence of imprisonment, petitioner was directed to pay a sum of Rs. 1 Lakh.

(iv) New Dimension in Restitutive Justice to Victim by Awarding Compensation out of Wages Earned by the Offender during the Imprisonment

Appreciating the new trend emerging in the field of victimology requiring amends by offender to victim or victims generally the three Judge bench of the Supreme Court consisting of M.M. Punchi, C.J. and K.T. Thomas and D.P. Wadhwa, JJ. took a novel step in *State of Gujarat* v. *Hon'ble High Court of Gujarat*.[80] The issue related to the payment of compensation to the victim of the crime or his family members out of wage earned in prison by the perpetrator of the crime by doing hard work pursuant to sentence of rigorous imprisonment awarded by the Court. In his leading judgment to which the other honourable justices accorded concurrence on the point, K.T. Thomas, J. expressed the sad affair of the effectiveness of section 357 of the Code of Criminal Procedure. The Court observed: "Section 357 Cr.P.C. has not proved to be of much effectiveness. Many persons who are sentenced to long-term imprisonment do not pay the compensation and instead they choose to continue in jail in default there of. It is only when fine alone is the sentence that the convicts invariably choose to remit the fine. But those are cases in which the harm inflicted on the victims would have been far less serious. Thus, the restorative and reparative theories are not translated into real benefits of the victims."[81]

The Supreme Court noted that the practice followed in many States, either by virtue of Jail rules or by convention is that (i) a portion of the money earned by the prisoner while working in imprison is sent to the dependents of the prisoner himself; (ii) and the balance, after deducting the amount expended by him for his extra expenses, is preserved to be disimbursed to him at the time of his release. The Court pointed out:

> "One area which is totally over looked in the above practice is the plight of the victims. Rehabilitation of the prisoner need not be by closing the eyes towards the suffering victims of the offence."

The Court suggested the States to adopt appropriate measures through law to ensure justice to the victims of crime. The Court opined that it is a constructive thinking for the State to make appropriate law for diverting some portion of the income earned by the prisoner when he is in jail to be paid to deserving victims.[82]

The Court felt constrained from issuing any direction to set apart any portion of the prisoner's earned wages for payment to the victim unless an appropriate law was enacted in this regard. It was so because of the interdict contained in Article 300-A of the Constitution which reads: "No person shall be deprived of his property save by authority of law." The Court, therefore, suggested that State concerned may bring about a legislation for that purpose.[83]

The Supreme Court issued a number of directions regarding payment of wages to prisoners according to the norm fixed by the wage-fixation body. The relevant direction for our present purpose reads as follow:

> "(5) We recommend to the State concerned to make law for setting apart a portion of the wages earned by the prisoner to be paid as compensation to deserving victims of the offence, the commission of which entitled the sentence of imprisonment to the prisoner, either directly or through a common fund to be created for this purpose or in any other feasible mode."

(v) New Rays of Hope in direction of Compensatory Justice to the Victims by Increasing Interest in use of Section 357(3)

The Supreme Court decision in *Harikishan* v. *Sukhvinder*[84] may be regarded as a land mark judgment recommending all criminal courts to award compensation to victims of crime against, person, property and reputation under Article 357(3) of the Code of Criminal Procedure. The facts of the case were like this. Harikishan was sitting near his tube-well. His son Joginder Singh and nephew Virendra Singh were sowing Berseem Crops. The accused armed with Ballams and Dangas came from the side of tube-well. One of the accused raised a Lalkara at which the accused attacked Joginder Singh and Virendra Singh. In the brawl that followed some of the accused were also injured. The trial Court convicted seven accused persons under Section 307 and 325 read with Sections 148 and 149 of the Indian Penal Code. On appeal the High Court acquitted two accused persons and convicted remaining five under sections 323/325 read with sections 148 and 149. But the High Court released all the accused on Probation and directed to pay Rs. 2,500 to Joginder Singh who was seriously injured. On appeal to the Supreme Court it was complained that Joginder Singh had sustained permanent disability due to head injuries and the amount of compensation was not adequate. The Supreme Court found that injuries were sustained from persons both the sides. The accused did not use sharp side of Ballam. They used only blunt side of it despite they being attacked by the other side. It indicated that they had no intention to commit murder. The Supreme Court did not find the case to fall under Section 307 and therefore, approved the benefit of probation to the accused. On the other hand it realized that the power of speech of Joginder Singh had been permanently impaired. His lifelong disability had to be taken care of. The Supreme Court consequently enhanced the amount of compensation to Rs. 50,000 as against the low figure of Rs. 2,500 awarded by the High Court. Shetty, J. pronouncing the two-Judge bench decision compared award of compensation under Section 357(1) and 357(3). The learned Judge pointed out that sub-section (1) of Section 357 provides power to award compensation on victims of the offence out of the sentence of fine imposed on accused. He exposed the non-use of sub-section (3) of Section 357. Said, the learned Judge:

> "Sub-Section (3) is an important provision but courts have seldom invoked it perhaps due to ignorance of the object of it."

The Court further elaborated:

> "It empowers the Court to award compensation to victims while passing judgment of conviction. In addition to conviction, the Court may order the accused to pay some amount by way of compensation to victim who has suffered by the action of accused."

The Court pointed out certain very basic and valuable points about sub-section (3) of Section 357 Cr.P.C. *Firstly*, it may be noted that the power of Courts to award compensation under sub-section (3) is not ancillary to other sentences but it is in addition to. *Secondly,* the power given to courts was intended to do something to assure the victim that he or she is not forgotten in the criminal justice system. *Thirdly,* it is a measure of responding appropriately to crime as well of reconciling the victim with the offender. It is, to some extent, a constructive approach to crime. It is indeed a step forward in our criminal justice system. *Fourthly,* the payment by way of compensation must, be reasonable. What is reasonable may depend upon the facts and circumstances of each case. The quantum of compensation may be determined by taking into account the nature of crime, the justness of claim by the victim and the ability of the accused to pay. If there are more than one accused they may be asked to pay in equal terms unless their capacity to pay varies considerably. The payment may also vary depending upon the acts of each accused. The reasonable period for payment of compensation, if necessary, by instalment, may also be given. The Court may enforce the order by imposing sentence in default.

The Supreme Court's verdict in relation to Section 357(3) is most welcome. But it does not mean that Section 357(3) is without limitations. *Firstly,* it is applicable only when sentence of fine is not imposed by the Court. In other words, it is applicable only in those cases wherein fine does not form it is applicable only in those cases wherein fine does not form part of the sentence. *Secondly,* the award of compensation is not mandatory. The use of word may in sub-section (3) of Section 357 indicates that it is discretionary on the Court to pass the compensation order or not to pass the order. *Thirdly,* the compensation order is dependent on the imposition sentence on conviction. If there is no conviction, there will be no order of compensation. *Fourthly,* state amendments adopt double standard. In favour of S.C.s and S.T.s victims compensation order is mandatory if accused be not of the same class. In matters of other victims it is discretionary.

There are many if and buts in relation to award of compensation. As discussed in relation to section 357(1), similar problems may arise as to effectiveness of compensation order. That is to say, it will depend on conviction of accused, capacity of offender to pay, apprehension and identification of the offender and realisation of the amount imposed by way of compensation. In no case state compensation or institutionalised form of compensation is to be awarded. In *State of M.P.* v. *Mangu*,[85] the Madhya Pradesh High Court made it clear that the Criminal Court while exercising jurisdiction under Section 357 of the Code cannot mulct the state with liability to pay compensation to the victim either temporarily or otherwise.

With a view to make the compensatory justice to victims more effective the Law Commission of India made certain welcome observations in its 84th Report. It reads:

(i) Section 357 of Cr.P.C., 1973, which talks of fining the accused, should be made more stringent so as to include the concept of compensation to victim.
(ii) In the case of custodial death two types of compensation were suggested to victim's family—one after the man is found guilty; and two, on a no-fault basis, as under Motor Vehicles Act.
(iii) The same should be extended to rape victim. The law should be suitably amended to incorporate this as well as right of inheritance for child born of rape.

The suitable move requires state liability through institutionalised compensation. It will form part of our study in the next chapter.

II. COMPENSATORY JUSTICE TO VICTIMS OF CRIME UNDER THE PROBATION OF OFFENDERS ACT

Section 3 of Probation of Offendenders Act, 1958 provides for release of offenders after admonition in cases in which crime is punishable with imprisonment for not more than two years or with fine or with both. Section 4 provides for probation in some more serious cases when offence is punishable with death or imprisonment for life but the Court is of opinion that having regard to the circumstances of the case including the nature of the offence and character of the offence, it is expedient to release him on probation of good conduct. The Court may instead of sentencing him at once to any punishment, direct that he be released on his entering into a bond with or without sureties. While exercising its power under Section 3 or 4 of the said Act the Court may in its discretion grant "reasonable compensation" to any person for loss of injury caused to him by commission of offence and cost of the proceedings.

Section 5(1) of the Probation of Offenders Act, 1958 provides for compensation. It reads as follow:

> *Power of the Court to Require Released Offender to Pay Compensation and Costs*—(1) The Court directing the release of an offender under section 3 or 4 may, if it think fit, make at the same time a further order directing him to pay:
>
> (a) such compensation as the Court thinks reasonable for loss or injury caused to any person by commission of the offence; and
>
> (b) such costs of the proceedings as the Court think reasonable.

Thus, the power to award compensation under the Probation of Offenders Act, is vested only with the Court releasing an offender and is purely in its discretion. In *Rajeshwari Prasad* v. *R.B. Gupta*[86] the Patna High Court expressed the view that the discretion of the trial Court is final. Even an appellate Court or High Court cannot interfere with exercise of the discretion by the Court unless it is of the view that such power has been exercised capriciously and unreasonably.

A comparison of Section 357 of the Code of Criminal Procedure, 1973 and Section 5 of the Probation of Offenders Act, 1954 have certain similarities. In both cases compensation may be granted for "any loss or injury" caused to a victim by the commission of the offence. In both the grant of compensation is discretionary. The striking dissimilarity between the two is that under Section 357 of Cr.P.C., an appellate Court, a High Court or Session Court may order payment of compensation in exercise of its power of revision. But Probation of Offenders Act neither confers such power to order compensation to the appellate courts nor allows them to interfere with the discretion of the Court releasing the offender after admotion or probation. Not only this award of compensation under section 357 of Cr.P.C. is related to impositions of fine. If no fine is imposed no compensation can be ordered. On the other hand, under Probation of Offenders Act compensation is not dependent on the imposition of fine. Furthermore, under Section 357(1)(a), (b) and (c) of the Cr.P.C. payment of compensation for any loss or injury caused by the offence can be ordered only when compensation, in opinion of the Court, is recoverable by such person in a civil court. In other words such payment is possible under Cr.P.C. only when the act forms both crime and tort. There is no such requirement under Section 5 of the Probation of Offenders Act.[87]

However, the award of compensation both under Section 357 of the Code of Criminal Procedure and Probation of Offenders Act being discretionary and providing no statutory right of the victim to be compensated lag behind the developments in this regard in western countries. To illustrate it the Russian Criminal Code 1960 imposes a duty on offender to make amends for the harm caused. On the other hand the French Code of Criminal Procedure allows injured person, as a matter of right, to join the criminal proceedings to claim compensation. Sections 104-107 of the Criminal Justice Act, 1988 of England imposes duty to award compensation and puts obligation to record reasons where the Court has power to do so and has not awarded such compensation.

III. COMPENSATORY JUSTICE TO VICTIMS UNDER CERTAIN OTHER STATUTORY PROVISIONS

There are a number of statutes—increasing day by day, which provide for Victims' compensation or assistance in one way or the other, though they are not in nature of criminal law like Cr.P.C. or Probation of Offenders Act. One of such

Acts has been referred to in Section 357 of the Code of Criminal Procedure itself, i.e. *Fatal Accidents Act 1855* (13 of 1855).[88] It provides for compensation to families (dependants) for the loss occasioned by the death of a person caused by an actionable wrong. Even before the speeding up of human face of justice to the victims during the 20th Century there were some legislations which provided for compensation to the victims of crimes, e.g. Opium Act, 1878; Cattle Trespass Act, 1871; The Police Act, 1861, the Personal Injuries (Emergency) Act, 1862; the Personal Injuries (Compensation Insurance) Act, 1850, etc.[89]

With the dawn of 20th Century and unprecedented events on world plane some of measures became imperative with view to provide security. *The Workmen's Compensation Act, 1923* was enacted with a view to provide compensation to workmen working in industry. There was no provision for compensation being paid to the workmen even in fatal cases. Had the employer been generous he could provide some amount by way of mercy. The workman could not claim compensation as a matter of right. The Act envisages to two types of victims of accidents while doing job. First are those cases where a workman meets with accident and dies. In such cases victims are dependents of the workman. The second category of cases are those where a workman meets with accident but survives with disabilities—total or partial, temporary or permanent. In either case section 3 and 10-A of the Workmen's Compensation Act, 1923 entitle the claimant in the event of death or bodily injury caused a workman by an accident arising out of and in the course of employment. The amount for different types of injuries sustained has been given in the Act itself.[90] For quick disposal of the claims Workmen Compensation Commissioner is appointed whose order of awarding compensation is final. Only one ground of substantial question of law an appeal may be preferred to the High Court under Section 30 of the said Act. The working and functioning of the Act is satisfactory and therefore most of the subsequent laws have incorporated its provisions in one way or the other. The speciality of the act is that for the first time it made departure from the basic principle of liability based on fault. In death cases it does not allow that principle of prevail and liability to pay compensation to the dependants is based on no-fault liability and is unaffected by the principles of assumed risks or contributory negligence.

Motor Vehicles Act, 1988 is another piece of law departing from the fault liability of tort. From time to time it was felt that the normal rule of tort based liability needed drastic change to provide justice to the victims of vehicular accidents. In *Kesavan Nair* v. *State Insurance Office*[91] Mr. Justice V.R. Krishna Iyer (as he then was) of Kerala High Court pointed out the existing lacuna in the following words:

> "Our sense of humanity and having due regard to the handicap of the innocent victim in establishing the negligence of the operator of the vehicle a blanket liability must be cast on the insurer, instead of its being restricted to cases where the vehicle operator has been shown to be negligent. This is more a matter for the legislature and not for the Court. But this is a lacuna in law which I think it would be just to rectify."

Again in *State of Haryana* v. *Darshana Devi,*[92] the same learned Judge (as Judge of Supreme Court) made strong plea of the principle of no-fault liability and on-the-spot settlement of claims to be adopted as the national policy.

In England Pearson Report, 1978 made it clear that "But' no-fault' compensation does not come from a source which necessarily had anything to do with causing the harm at all, *with or without fault*. It has been described as compensation obtainable without proving fault and outside the tort system."

Section 140, Motor Vehicles Act, 1988 gives statutory basis to the liability to pay compensation in certain cases on the principle of no fault. It fixes Rs. 50,000 as compensation for death and 25,000 for permanent disablement. The claimant has not to prove that death or permanent disablement was due to any wrongful act, neglect or default of the owner or owners of the vehicle or vehicles concerned or any other person. No contributory negligence plea will affect the amount of compensation or liability to pay compensation. Section 140 does not discharge of liability of the owner of the vehicle. He will also be responsible to pay compensation payable under section 163-A of the Act.

Thus, Motor Vehicles (Amendment) Act, 1994 added Section 163-A based on no liability principle giving option to the victim/claimant to claim compensation as indicated in the Second Schedule. It provides for assessment of the amount of compensation on the basis of annual income and age multiplier.

Thus at present a claimant can claim compensation on the basis of no-fault liability either under section 140 or under 163-A. Though both sections are based on non-fault liability, the difference between the two are as follows:

(i) Under Section 140 compensation is payable, apart from death only in case of permanent disablement. Under Section 163-A a compensation is payable for death or injury irrespective of its consequence, i.e. resulting a permanent disablement or not.

(ii) Under Section 140 sums for two eventualities are fixed, i.e. Rs. 50,000 for death and Rs. 25,000 for permanent injury.
Under Section 163-A the compensation is payable on a structured formula basis as indicated in the Second Schedule depending on the age and income of the accident victim.

(iii) Under Section 140 amount for death is a flat sum of Rs. 50,000
Under Section 163-A Rs. 50,000 is minimum. It may go up to 8,00,000 depending on the age and income of the victim.

(iv) Under Section 140 in case of death a fixed amount of Rs. 50,000 is payable and nothing more.
Under Section 163-A other fixed sums are payable towards funeral expenses, loss of consortium, loss of estate, and actual medical expenses incurred before death.

(v) Under Section 140 there is a provision for fixed amount of Rs. 25,000 in the case of permanent disablement, if injury does not result into permanent disablement there is no provision for payment.

> Under Section 163-A compensation is payable depending on the percentage of loss of earning capacity. In addition, certain fixed amounts are payable for pain and suffering, actual medical expenses and actual income lost.

A claimant can claim compensation on no-fault liability either under Section 140 or Section 163-A. An additional right to claim compensation on fault liability is open as earlier under Section 165.[93] If the owner is liable to pay compensation under Section 165, he can deduct such amount from the compensation payable by him either under Section 140 or under Section 163-A.

A victim/claimant can file a claim for compensation before a duly constituted Motor Accident Claims Tribunal. Provision has also been made empowering the Government to establish and administer a solatium fund of which compensation can be paid in cases of death or grievous injury resulting in *hit and run* cases when the person guilty of causing the accident remains untraced.

The Public Liability Insurance Act, 1991 was passed with object to providing immediate relief to person affected by accident occurring while handling any hazardous substances. The owner of hazardous substances are mandatorily required to take out insurance policy. The Act is based on liability without fault. It provides for victims of hazardous substances who are persons other than workmen. It was felt necessary because workmen and employees of hazardous installations are protected under separate laws but members of public are not assured of any relief except through long legal process of litigation. Growth of hazardous industries is growing risks from accidents not only to workmen but also to the innocent members of the public who may be living in vicinity. The following persons are authorised to make an application for claiming relief under the Act.

(i) Any person who has sustained injury due to accident occurring while handling hazardous substance;

(ii) Any owner of the property which has been

damaged by an accident occurring while handling hazardous substance;

(iii) Any or all of the legal representatives of the deceased where death has resulted from the accident occurring while handling hazardous substance; or

(iv) Any agent duly authorised by such all or any of the legal representatives of the deceased.

Section 3(1) read with the Scheduled of the Public Liability Insurance Act, 1991 provide for the following monetary relief to the victims of accidents occurring while handling hazardous substance.

(1) Reimbursement of medical expenses incurred upto a maximum of Rs. 12,500 in each case.

(2) For the fatal accidents the relief will be Rs. 25,000 per person in addition to reimbursement of medical expenses, if any, incurred on the victims upto a maximum of Rs. 12,500.

(3) For permanent total or permanent partial disability or other injury or sickness, the relief will be: (a) reimbursement of medical expenses incurred if any, upto a maximum of Rs. 12,500 in each case, and (b) cash relief on the basis of percentage of disablement as certified by an authorised physician. The relief for total permanent disability will be Rs. 25,000.

(4) For loss of wages due to temporary partial disability which reduces the earning capacity of the victim, there will be a fixed monthly relief not exceedings Rs. 1000 per month upto a maximum of 3 months; provided the victim has been hospitalized for a period exceeding 3 days and is above 16 years of age.

(5) Upto Rs. 6,000 depending on the actual damage, for any damage to private party.

The range of victim has been broadened further by the United Nations Conference on Environment and Development held at Rio-de-Janerio in June, 1992. It called upon the States to develop National laws regarding liability and compensation for the victims of pollution and other environmental damage. India had participated in it and in response to its commitment, it enacted *The National Environment Tribunal Act, 1995.* Section 3(1) provides for liability to pay compensation in certain cases on principle of no fault. It reads: "where death or injury to, any person (other than a workman) or damage to any property or environment has resulted from an accident, the owner shall be liable to pay compensation for such death, injury or damage under all or any of heads specified in the schedule." The schedule enumerates 14 heads ranging from death to loss of business or employment.

There are certain Statues which do not provide for compensation to the victims. For example, *Protection of Civil Rights Act, 1955* provides for punishment for offences arising out of untouchability[94] but it does not provide for compensation to the victim, even though punishment may include fine and State is empowered to impose collective fine.[95] So is the case with *The Scheduled Castes and the Scheduled Tribes (Prevention of Atrocities) Act, 1989.* It provides for punishment for offences and atrocities in which fine is included.[96] It also empowers State Government to impose collective fine like Section 10-A of Protection of Civil Rights Act. But it does not provide for compensation to the victim of crimes. However, the S.C. and S.T. (Prevention of Atrocities) Rules, 1995 provides for assistance programme.[97] Rule 11 provides for traveling allowance, daily allowance, maintenance expenses and transport facilities to the victim of atrocity or his or her dependents and witnesses. Rule 14 requires that the State Government shall make necessary provisions in its annual budget for providing relief and rehabilitation facilities to the victims of atrocities.[98] Rule 15 speaks of contingency plan by the State Government containing a package of relief measures including the following:

(a) scheme to provide immediate relief in cash or in kind or both;

(b) allotment of agricultural land and house-sites;
(c) scheme for employment in Government or Government Undertaking to the dependant or one of the family members of the victim;
(d) pension scheme for widows, dependants children of the deceased, handicapped or old age victim of atrocities;
(e) mandatory compensation for the victims;
(f) scheme for strengthening the socio-economic condition of the victim;
(g) provisions for providing brick/stone masonry house to the victims; and
(h) such other elements as health care, supply of essential commodities, electrification, adequate drinking water facility, burial cremation ground and link roads to the Scheduled Castes and the Scheduled Tribes habitants.

With increasing incidents of domestic violence Parliament has enacted the *Protection of Women from Domestic Violence Act, 2005.* This Act does not directly define the victim. Rather it uses and defines "aggrieved person" which means any woman who is, or has been, in a domestic relationship with the respondent and who alleges to have been subjected to any act of domestic violence by the respondent. This Act guarantees victims of domestic violence right to get compensation for any physical or mental injury or any other monetary loss due to domestic violence. Section 22 of the Act deals with compensation orders passed by the Magistrate for injuries including mental torture and emotional distress caused by the acts of domestic violence committed by the defendant and section 20 entitles to get certain other monetary relief to victim to meet the expenses incurred and losses suffered including loss of earnings, medical expenses, loss of property and maintenance of the victim and her children. Section 23 empowers Magistrate to pass interim order. Section 18 empowers Magistrate to pass protection orders in favour of victim and prohibits the respondent from committing any act of domestic violence; aiding or abetting in the commission of acts of domestic violence; entering the place of employment of the aggrieved person/victim; alienating any assets, operating bank lockers of bank accounts operated jointly, etc. Section 19 empowers Magistrate to pass residence orders in favour of victim.

The wide range of compensatory justice also covers some other Acts like Consumer Protection Act, 1986, The Right to Information Act, 2005. The former allows compensation in cases of deficient services including medical services to the patients and latter allows the citizen's right of information against the police and the court. A against police victim has right of information in respect of lodging of F.I.R., investigating process and its outcome. Against court he has right to information with respect to progress of the case, outcomes of case in connection with inquiry, issue of process, trial, sentencing, etc.

IV. JUSTICE TO THE VICTIMS AND MALIMATH COMMITTEE REPORT

It is felt that Indian legislative efforts are not very much inspiring so far as victims role in administration of criminal Justice is concerned. The criminal justice system (CJS) warrants two things: *First,* compensation for loss suffered, and physical, mental or emotional injury sustained by victim; and *Second,* effective participation of the victim in the criminal justice process.

The State has duty to protect the rights of the innocent and punish the guilty. In pursuit of these duties, Ministry of Home Affairs (Government of India) constituted the committee on reforms of criminal justice system. The committee was constituted under chairmanship of Justice Dr. V.S. Malimath. The reference was made to make comprehensive examination of all the functionaries of criminal justice system, the fundamental principles and the relevant laws. Conceding and pointing out that justice to victims is one of the inseparable imperatives of the criminal justice in India. The committee realised that victims had certain advantageous position in inquisitorial system of criminal trials prevailing in France, Germany and other continental countries. Under our system of accusatorial or adversial system fair trial and fairness to the accused is better protected. Anyway, some good features of the inquisitorial system can be adopted to strengthen the adversial system with a view to make it more effective.

The good features of inquisitorial system include: (1) the duty of the court to search for truth; (2) to assign pro-active roles to the judges; (3) to give directions to the investigating officers and prosecution agencies in the matter of investigation and leading evidence with the object of seeking the truth and focusing on Justice to victims.

For our present study recommendations of the Malimath Committee relating to 'Justice to Victims of Crime' are relevant. The important recommendations in respect of justice to victims are as follow:

(i) The victim, and if he is dead, his legal representative shall have the right to be impleaded as a party in every criminal proceeding where the offence is punishable with seven years imprisonment or more.

(ii) In select cases notified by the appropriate Government, with the permission of the court an approved voluntary organization shall have the right to be impleaded in court proceedings.

(iii) The victim has a right to be represented by an advocate of his choice; provided that an advocate shall be provided at the cost of the State if the victim is not in a position to afford a lawyer.

(iv) The victim's right to participate in criminal trial shall, *inter alia,* include—

- (a) To produce evidence, oral or documentary, with leave of the court and/or to seek directions for production of such evidence.
- (b) To ask questions to the witnesses or to suggest to the court questions which may be put to witnesses.
- (c) To know the status of investigation and to move the court to issue directions for further investigation on certain matters or to a

supervisory officer to ensure effective and proper investigation to assist in the search for truth.

(d) To be heard in respect of the grant or cancellation of bail.

(e) To be heard whenever Prosecution seeks to withdraw and to offer to continue the prosecution.

(f) To advance arguments after the Prosecutor has submitted arguments.

(g) To participate in negotiations leading to settlement of compoundable offences.

(v) The victim shall have a right to prefer an appeal against any adverse order passed by the court acquitting the accused, convicting for a lesser punishment offence, imposing inadequate sentence or granting inadequate compensation. Such appeal shall lie to the court to which an appeal ordinarily lies against the order of conviction of such court.

(vi) Legal services to victims in select crimes may be extended to include psychiatric and medical help, interim compensation and protection against secondary victimization.

(vii) Victim compensation is a State obligation in all serious crimes, whether the offender is apprehended or not, convicted or acquitted. This is to be organized in a separate legislation by Parliament. The draft bill on the subject submitted to government in 1995 by the Indian Societies of Victimology provides a tentative framework for consideration.

(viii) The victim compensation law will provide for the creation of a victim compensation fund to be administered possibly by the Legal Services Authority. The law should provide for the scale of compensation in different offences for the guidance of the court. It may specify offences in which compensation may not be granted and conditions under which it may be awarded or withdrawn.

In addition to the victim's right, the committee recommended the rights and duties of witnesses, investigating agencies (investigations wing to be separated from law and order wing); prompt registration of criminal cases; refusal to entertain complaints regarding commission of crime to be made punishable; treatment of witness with courtesy and dignity along with facilities; traveling allowances and D.A. to be paid; protection to the families of witnesses should be given and judges to be vigilant and regulate cross-examination to prevent witnesses being subjected to harassment, annoyance and indignity.

A detailed account of recommendation on these points is contained in para 2 to 13 of the recommendation which reads as follow:

1. Rights and duties of the complainant/informant, the victim, the accused, the witnesses and the authorities to whom they can approach with their grievances should be incorporated in separate schedules to the Code. They should be translated in the respective regional languages and made available free of cost to the citizens in the form of easily understandable pamphlets.

   Police is the first pillar of criminal justice system besides 'prosecution and defense', and (criminal) courts. The machinery of criminal justice system is put into gear when an offence is registered and then investigated. A prompt and quality investigation is therefore the foundation of the effective criminal justice. Victim's first interaction is with the police while setting the criminal law in motion. So police must play sympathetic and sensitizing role against victim, in addition to performing its primary duty to help him getting justice. The Committee made several recommendations as to police system. Some of important suggestions are as follow:
2. The Investigation Wing should be separated from the Law and Order Wing (As it will promote fair and expeditious investigation which might help victims).

3. Criminal cases should be registered promptly with utmost promptitude by Station House Officers (SHOs). and, stringent punishment should be provided for false registration of cases and false complaints. Section 182/211 of IPC be suitably amended.
4. Suitable amendments be made to remove the distinction between cognizable and non-cognizable offences in relation to the power of the police to investigate offences and to make it obligatory on the police officer to entertain complaints regarding commission of all offences and to investigate them.
5. Refusal to entertain complaints regarding commission of any offence shall be made punishable.
6. Similar amendment shall be made in respect of offences under special laws.

   The prospect of vitim's success is dependent upon the active role of witnesses. It is the pressing need that criminal justice should also focus on position of witnesses in existing scenario, and it should aim at elevating the status of witnesses. To meet this end, the Committee recommended that—
7. (a) Witness who comes to assist the court should be treated with dignity and shown due courtesy. An official should be assigned o provide assistance to him.

   (b) Separate place should be provided with proper facilities such as seating, resting, toilet, drinking water, etc. for the convenience of the witnesses in the court premises.
8. Rates of traveling and other allowances to the witness should be reviewed so as to compensate him for the expenses that he incurs. Proper arrangements should be made for payment of the allowances due to the witness on the same day when the case is adjourned without examining the witness he should be paid T.A. and D.A. the same day.

9. A law should be enacted for giving protection to the witnesses and their family members on the lines of the laws in USA and other countries.
10. Courts should list the cases in such a manner as to avoid the witnesses being required to come again and again for giving evidence.
11. The witness should be provided a seat for him to sit down and given evidence in the court.
12. The judge should be vigilant and regulate cross-examination to prevent the witness being subjected to harassment, annoyance or indignity.

The Committee has recommended for the right of victim/complainant and in case of his death, of his legal representatives (LRs) as well as voluntary organization to actively participate in criminal trial. Such a provision will lead to media and public trial of an accused which will check biased court trial. and victim will get a fair chance to put his side. In existing CJS victim's role is only as a prosecuting witness. But Committee's suggestion as to victim's right participation in criminal trial will strengthen his status, and enable him to ensure justice done.

Further, the Committee has rightly recommended for having/enacting a victim compensatory law. Though compensation is also granted under the present system of CJS, it is given generally only in the cases of crime against women, against SC/STS or crimes relating to police atrocities or abuse of power. Such a law should be enacted so that the victims of crimes of should not feel deprived of their life and liberty and should also not feel to have been discarded by the society.

Deliberations of the Committee recognized that 'victims at present do not get legal rights and protection they deserve to play their just role in criminal proceedings'. The Committee suggested interaction between the police, the judges, the prosecution and defense lawyers, jail officials and the general public so as to remove the defects in the existing system. It exposed that 'the system is unlikely to restore the balance as fair procedure in the pursuit of truth'.

Referring to S. 357 of the CrPC, 1973, the Committee said:

"Not only was the victim's right to compensation ignored except a token provision under the criminal procedure code but also the right to participate as the dominant stakeholder in criminal proceedings was taken away from him... The principle of compensating victims of crime has for long been recognized by the law though it is recognized more as a token relief rather than part of a punishment or substantial remedy."

In the backdrop of the Constitutional spirit displayed by the Apex Court in its celebrated judicial pronouncements98 for protecting the basic rights of, and ensuring justice to victims of crime, the Committee emphasized to have a comprehensive Victim-Compensatory Scheme modeled on the Victim Compensation Bill, 1995, proposed by the Indian Society of Victimology and submitted to the Government of India. But surprisingly it did not chalk out the scheme on the pattern of 1995 Bill for compensating the victims of crime. The main and noticeable defect of the Malimath Committee report is that it did not pay much heed to victim compensatory model suggested under the 156th Report of the Law Commission of India which had chalked out a good model by suggesting insertion of Section 357-A in Cr.P.C., 1973. It read interalia:

"S. 357-A. Victim Compensation Scheme—

(1) Every State Government in co-ordination with the Central Government shall prepare a Scheme for providing funds for the purpose of compensating the victim or his dependents who have suffered loss or injury as a result of the crime and who require rehabilitation.

(2) Under the Scheme the District Legal Services Authority at the district level and the State Legal Services Authority at the State level shall decide the quantum of compensation to be awarded whenever the trial court to that effect makes a recommendation.

(3) If the trial court, at the conclusion of the trial, is satisfied that the compensation awarded under Section 357(3) is not adequate for such rehabilitation, or where the cases end in acquittal or discharge and the victim has to be rehabilitated, it may recommend to the District Legal Services Authority if the compensation in its view is less than Rs. 30,000 or to the State Legal Services Authority if the compensation is more than Rs. 30,000.

(4) Where the offender is not traced or identified, but the victim is identified, and where no trial takes place it is open to the victim or his dependents to make and application under sub-section (2) to the District Legal Services Authority at the district level and the State Legal Services Authority at the state level for award of compensation.

(5) On receipt of such recommendations or on the applications under sub-section (4), as the case may be, the District Legal Services Authority or the State Legal Services Authority, as the case may be, shall after due enquiry award adequate compensation by completing the enquiry within two months.

(6) District Legal Services Authority or the State Legal Services Authority, as the case may be, to alleviate the suffering of the victim may order immediate first aid facilities or for medical benefits to made available free of cost on the certificate of the Police Officer not below the rank of the Officer-in-Charge of the Police State or a Magistrate of the area concerned or any other interim relief as the appropriate authority deems fit."

Another model was suggested by the National Law School of India University Bill (NLSIU Bill) (called as Victims (Criminal Injuries) Right to Assistance Bill, 1996), which provided for creation of 'Crime Assistance Fund' at the National, State and District levels to render assistance to crime victims and their dependents.

In spite of some defects in the Report a perusal of recommendations of the Malimath Committee reveals that it, like the Law Commission, strongly felt that compensating victims of crime is a state obligation, whether the offender is apprehended or not, convicted or acquitted. Keeping in view this end, it proposes a 'victim Compensation Fund' to be possibly administered by the Legal Services Authorities created under Legal Services Authority Act, 1987; (ii) the scale of compensation is different offences for the guidance of the court; and (iii) the categories of offences in which compensation cannot be granted as well as the conditions under which it can be awarded or withdrawn. A 'Victim Compensation Fund', according to the Committee, as was also suggested by the Law Commission, be generated by pulling together 'fines' recovered, 'funds' generated by the criminal justice system and solicited 'public contributions.' Even if part of the assets confiscated and forfeited in organized crime and financial frauds is made part of the fund and if it is managed efficiently, there will be no paucity of resources for compensating victims of crime. In any case the Committee asserted that in dispensing justice to victims of crime, the scarcity of resources should not come in the way.

The merit of the Malimath Committee lies in the fact that it, for the first time, delved into the 'participation' of victims in criminal process as an inseparable component of justice to victims and suggested a set of recommendations for their effective participation. The criminal justice system in India, the Committee felt, and rightly so, exhibited its utter insensitivity to victims of crime by denying them the right to participate, except as witnesses in criminal proceedings and by not giving them an opportunity to assist criminal courts by adducing evidence or putting questions to witnesses. The Committee appears to support inquisitorial procedure and taking inspiration from the French victim participatory criminal justice system it observed:

> "His (victim's) active participation during trial will be great help in the search for truth without inconveniencing the Prosecution. He can supplement the evidence adduced by the Prosecution and put forth

his own arguments. He will be of help to the court in the matter of deciding the grant or cancellation of bail. He will adduce evidence in the matter of loss, pain and suffering to decide on his entitlement of interim relief and compensation by way of restitution. Wrongful attempts to withdraw or close the prosecution due to extraneous factors can be resisted if the court were to have continued assistance of the victim. For all these reasons and more, it is clear that if the criminal proceedings have to be fair to both the parties and if the court were to be properly assisted in its search for truth, the law has to recognize the right of victim's participation in investigation, prosecution and trial."

There appear to be good points in the Report of Committee, especially with respect to the following:

(1) To produce evidence, oral or documentary, with the leave of the court and/or to seek directions for production of such evidence.
(2) To put questions to witnesses or to suggest to the court questions which may be put to witnesses.
(3) To know the status of investigation and to move the court to issue directions for further investigation on certain matters or to a supervisory officer to ensure effective and proper investigation to assist in the search for truth.
(4) To be heard in respect of the grant or cancellation of bail.
(5) To be heard whenever Prosecution seeks to withdraw and to offer to continue the prosecution.
(6) To advance arguments after the Prosecutor has submitted arguments.
(7) To participate in negotiations leading to settlement of compoundable offences.
(8) To prefer an appeal against any adverse order passed by a court acquitting the accused, convicting for a lesser offence, imposing inadequate sentence, or granting inadequate compensation.

The Malimath Committee has not attracted much appreciations. But with a view to make Indian march towards ensuring justice to victims *on par* with developed countries enactment of compensatory law, ensuring victim compensation even in cases of unidentified and unapprehanded offenders and constitution of victim compensation fund need serious consideration and implementation.

Notes and References

1. Vibhute, K.I., Book Review of Mundarthi, Sammaiah, 'Law on Compensation to Victims of Crime and Abuse of Power', 46 JILI (2004) 594 at 595 Prof. Vibhute does not appreciate inclusion of Sections 237, 250, 358 and 359 of Cr.P.C. into compensatory scheme like section 357.
2. Statutory provisions other than those contained in Cr.P.C. or Probation of Offenders Act, that is to say, Fatal Accidents Act, Motor Vehicles Act, Consumer Protection Act, the Workmen's Compensation Act, the Protection of Women From Domestic Violence Act, The S.C.S.T. (Prevention of Atrocities) Act, etc.
3. Section 237, Cr. P.C., 1973.
4. Section 250.
5. Section 265-A inserted by Act 2 of 2006 (w.e.f. 5.7.2006).
6. Section 358.
7. Section 359.
8. 42nd Report, Law Commission of India.
9. Quoted in Joga Rao, S.V., Victim Restitution, The Lawyer 1990 (June) system (1997), pp. 92-93.
10. Sections mentioned are 298, 333, 334, 341, 342, 352, 355, 358, 426, 427, 447, 448, 491, 497, 498, 500, 501, 502, 504, 506 and 508.
11. Section 320(2) has the table consisting of offences under sections 324, 325, 335, 337, 338,343, 344, 346, 354, 357, 379, 381, 403, 406, 407, 408, 411, 414, 417, 418, 419, 420, 421, 422, 423, 424, 428, 429, 430, 451, 582, 483, 486, 494, 500 and 509.
12. (1999) 5 S.C.C. 238 at p. 240.
13. I.L.R. 41 Mad. 685.
14. Aslam Meah *v.* Emperor, I.L.R. 45 Cal. 817.
15. 1999 Cr. L.J. 117 (Gau.).
16. A.I.R. 1922 Cal. 191, also Emperor *v.* Bhailal, A.I.R. 1929 Nag. 278.
17. 1999 Cr. L.J. 112 (J.K.)
18. *Ibid.*, p. 1122.
19. (2005) I.S.C.C. 347; JT (1987) 2 S.C. 361 decided on April 29, 1987.
20. A.I.R. 1978 S.C. 1452.

21. *Ibid.*
22. 1992 Cr. L.J. 749.
23. 1993 Cr. L.J. 2076 (Raj.).
24. 1996 Cr.L.J. 3103 (Kent.).
25. 1996 Cr.L.J. 2973 (A.P.)
26. (2005) I.S.C.C. 343.
27. (1973) 2 S.C.C. 456.
28. 2005) I.S.C.C. 347; J.T. (1987) 2 S.C. 361.
29. (1990) Supp. S.C.C. 681.
30. (1999) 2 S.C.C. 213.
31. (2005) I.S.C. 343.
32. (1999) 5 S.C.C. 238.
33. *Supra* f.n. 27.
34. *Supra* f.n. 31.
35. *Supra* f.n. 30.
36. *Supra* f.n. 28.
37. *Supra* f.n. 29.
38. Section 482: *Saving of inherent powers of High Court*: "Nothing in this Code shall be deemed to limit or affect the inherent powers of the High Court to make such orders as may be necessary to give effect to any order under this Code or to prevent abuse of the process of any Court or otherwise to secure the ends of justice."
39. Article 142, The Constitution of India reads. "(1) The Supreme Court in the exercise of its jurisdiction may pass such decrees or make such order as is necessary for doing *complete justice* in any cause or matter pending before it, and any decree so passed or so made shall be enforceable throughout the territory of India in such manner as may be prescribed by or under any law made by Parliament and, until provision in that behalf is so made; in such manner as the President may by order prescribe"
40. *Supra* f.n. 31.
41. 1980 Cr.L.J. 514 (Guj.).
42. (1978) M.L.J. (Knt.)
43. Sub-clause (2) of section 250 Cr. P.C., 1973.
44. Sub-clause (3).
45. Sub-clause (4).
46. Sub-clause (5).
47. Proviso to sub-clause (5).
48. Sub-clause (6).
49. Sub-clause (7).
50. Sub-clause (8).
51. Saleh *v.* Emperor, A.I.R. 1932 Sind. 156.
52. Ram Lubhaya *v.* Jaga Nath 30 P.L.R. 361.
53. I.L.R. 38 Mad. 1091.
54. Chorbyn *v.* Ameer Khan 21 P.R. 1859 Cr.

55. Crown *v.* Debi Buksh 25 P.R. 1868 Cr.
56. (1999) 8 S.C.C. 638; The Court also referred to the earlier cases decided by it in which "plea bargaining" had been disallowed. Such cases include Madan Lal Ramchandra Daga *v.* State of Maharashtra, A.I.R. 1968. S.C. 1267; Murlidhar Meghraj Loya *v.* State of Maharashtra (1976) 3 S.C.C. 684; Ganeshmal Jashraj *v.* Govt. of Gujarat (1980) 1 S.C.C. 363; Thippaswamy *v.* State of Karnataka (1983) 1 S.C. 194 and Kasambhai Abdulrehman bhai Sheikh *v.* State of Gujarat (1980) 3 S.C.C. 120.
57. J.M. Mohammad Cassim *v.* G.S.J. Sheikh Thamby Sahib, A.I.R. 1940 Rang. 33.
58. Sub-section (2) of Section 357.
59. Sub-section (4) of Section 357.
60. As quoted in Joga Rao, Victim Restitution, *The Lawyer*, June 1990, p. 18.
61. The Law Commission of India, Forty-First Report: The Code of Criminal Procedure, Vol. I (1969), p. 356.
62. (1976) 78 P.L.R. 867.
63. A.I.R. 1952 S.C. 14.
64. A.I.R. 1977 S.C. 1323.
65. A.I.R. 1978 S.C. 1525.
66. *Ibid.*
67. A.I.R. 1989 S.C. 1661.
68. A.I.R. 1989 S.C. 1822.
69. A.I.R. 1989 S.C. 1661.
70. A.I.R. 1989 S.C. 1822.
71. A.I.R. 1989 S.C. 1661.
72. A.I.R. 1989 S.C. 1822.
73. A.I.R. 1977 S.C. 892.
74. A.I.R. 1995 S.C. 1177.
75. A.I.R. 1995 S.C. 2452.
76. A.I.R. 1995 S.C. 1935.
77. 1996(1) Crimes 88 (A.P.)
78. (2004) 10 S.C.C. 177.
79. 1996(1) Crime 100 (Kerala): 1996 Cr.L.J. 143 (Ker.)
80. (1998) 7 S.C.C. 392.
81. *Ibid.*, (para 48), p. 412.
82. *Ibid.*, (para 49), p. 412.
83. *Ibid.*, para (50), pp. 412-13.
84. A.I.R. 1988 S.C. 2127.
85. 1995(4) Crimes 818 (M.P.).
86. A.I.R. 1961 Pat. 19.
87. Das Bharat B.; *Victims in the Criminal Justice System* (1997), p. 76.
88. *Ibid.*, 77.
89. Professor K.I. Vibhute disputes such enactments being put under

"Compensation to Victims of Crime." See Prof. K.L. Vishute's Book Review of Sammaiah Mundrathi, Law on Compensation To Victims of Crime and Abuse of Power *(2002) 46 JILI (2004) 594* at p. 596.

90. Section 143, Motor Vehicles Act, 1988 and Section 3(2) Explanation (i), The National Environment Tribunal Act, 1995.
91. 1971 ACJ 219 (Ker.).
92. (1979) 2 S.C.C. 236.
93. Sreenath M.R. and Sreenath Lalitha, *Law Relating to Compensation under Motor Vehicles Act*, Eastern Book Company, Lucknow.1998/
94. Sections 3, 4, 5, 6, 7 and 7A, Protection of Civil Rights Act, 1955.
95. Section 10-A.
96. Section 3, The S.C. and S.C. (Prevention of Atrocities) Act, 1989.
97. Section 16.
98. Khatri *v.* State of Bihar, A.I.R. 1981 S.C. 928; Rudal Shah *v.* State of Bihar, A.I.R. 1983 S.C. 1086; Nilabati Behera *v.* State of Orissa, A.I.R. 1993 S.C. 1960.

6

Activist Judicial Role in Awarding Compensation to Victims as a Public Law Remedy

In wake of new emerging forces putting threat to life, liberty and property of individual in the society the range of victimology and ways to ensure justice to the victims is also widening day-by-day. The most effective and recent comer in the field is the concept of public law remedy. The Constitutional law and administrative law make up the basic content of what is called public law. Constitutional law is the law governing the organisation and operation of the State. Administrative law is the law governing the organisation and operation of the administrative branch of the government and the relations of the administration with the legislature, the judiciary and the public.[1]

The development of the concept of victimology and State's concern to ensure safety and security to the people is pointer to the responsibility of the State. As senator Mike Mansfield once introducing a bill in Senate to compensate victims of crime said, "the point has reached where we must give consideration to the victims of crime—to the one who suffers because of crime—society has an obligation, when the protection of society is not sufficient to prevent a person from being victimized, society then has an obligation to compensate the victim for the failure of protection."[2] At present time there are many ways through which people may be victimized or affected. They may fall prey of State police and army or other officials. They may fall prey of riots, terrorism and so on so forth. The public law remedy has been evolved to provide for compensation as a remedy or redressal.

The process of ensuring compensatory justice to the victims by way of public law remedy is peculiar and novel in itself. It is peculiar in the sense that it will not come in the way of the aggrieved person claiming additional compensation in a civil court, in enforcement of the private law remedy in tort, nor come in the way of criminal court ordering compensation under Section 357[3] of the Code of Criminal Procedure.

Since the existing statutory remedies in India are not adequate to provide safeguards to the victims of crime and with the cases of increasing state lawlessness and state violence have proved to be less effective in compensating the victims of the abuse of power, the public law remedy with added dimension of public interest litigation and liberalizing *locus standi* is most welcome for adequately and effectively compensating the victims of abuse of power. The higher judiciary's crusade to wipe out tears from the victims' eyes is not limited to the issue to compensatory orders against the State, it also includes issue of direction against individual for violation of the right under Article 21. Thus, the Supreme Court has introduced a new concept in compensatory justice jurisprudence in the domain of public law by holding an individual liable for violating Article 21 and treating it amendable to writ jurisdiction.[4] Not only this, the judiciary has taken care of not only abuses of State power and violence, but it has also taken care of failure on the part of State to save life of individual during riot or other mishaps.

The study of this chapter is devoted to the different types of situations affecting victims of the abuse of power or putting threat to life, atrocities, etc. and awarding compensation to the victims therefor.

(I) COMPENSATORY JUSTICE IN CASES OF ILLEGAL ARREST AND UNWARRANTED DETENTION

The Supreme Court of India has articulated the concept of compensatory jurisprudence for the flagrant violation of fundamental rights of people implicit in Article 21. This view of the Court was evolved for the first time in *Rudal Shah* v. *State of Bihar.*[5] Rudal Shah was acquitted by the Session Court on June 3, 1968 but remained in jail due to the irresponsible behaviour of state officers. A *habeas corpus* petition was filed under Article 32 of the Constitution and prayer was made for his release and compensation for illegal detention. Rudal Shah was released on October 16, 1982 after the lapse of 14 years. The Supreme Court awarded Rs. 30,000 as interim compensation in addition to the sum of Rs. 5,000 already paid by the government. While delivering the judgment the Supreme Court made a departure from its traditional pattern of practice and pointed out the reasons behind it. It said:

> "Article 21 of the Constitution guaranteeing the fundamental right of life and liberty would loose its significance if the powers of Supreme Court were limited to passing orders for release from illegal detention; and the Court refused to order compensation it will be doing a mere lip service to his fundamental right to liberty which the State Government has so grossly violated."[6]

The Supreme Court order of release and award of compensation was in the nature of a palliative and it does not preclude the petitioner from bringing a suit to recover appropriate damages from State and erring officers. The decision of the Supreme Court is most welcome and sowed seed of future expansion of new remedies in its original jurisdiction under Article 32 of the Constitution for the vindication of fundamental rights. Just after the twelve days of the pronouncement of the Supreme Court Judgment in *Rudal Shah's* case the Supreme Court directed the Bihar State Government to pay a sum of Rs. 15,000 to Oraon in *Boma Charan Oraon* v. *State of Bihar.*[7] In the instant (unreported) case Oraon had been illegally kept in Ranchi mental asylum over six years, even after he had been certified as fit for discharge. Thus, the Division Bench of the Supreme Court consisting of P.N. Bhagwati and S. Mukherji, JJ. expanded the claim of compensation to person illegally detained treating it as violation of personal liberty under Article 21 of the Constitution.

On 10.4.1991, the Madras High Court awarded a compensation of Rs. 25,000 to Murugan a fifteen years old boy who had been detained for nearly a month in a police state and was tortured and according to the boy's testimony he was compelled to consume arrack Ganja and human waste diluted in water.[8]

In *Bhim Singh* v. *State of Jammu and Kashmir*,[9] Bhim Singh, President of Panther Party while in way to attend the session of J. and K. Legislative Assembly as its member was arrested and detained in police custody deliberately to prevent him from attending session of Legislative Assembly. The police officers arrested deliberately and *mala fide* and Magistrate and Sub-Judge aided them either by colluding with them or by their casual attitude.

Awarding a compensation of Rs. 50,000 to the petitioner for violation of his constitutional right of personal liberty under Article 21 of the Constitution, O. Chinnappa Reddy, J. observed:

> "When a person comes to us with the complaint that he has been arrested and imprisoned with mischievious or malicious intent and that his constitutional and legal rights were invaded, the mischief or malice and the invasion may not be washed away or wished away by his being set free. In appropriate cases, we have the jurisdiction to compensate the victim by awarding suitable momentary compensation."[10]

The Supreme Court observed further that the custodial law and order should not become depredators of civil liberties. Their duty is to protect not abduct. The message of *Bhim Singh's case* is that compensation is awardable not only in cases of total deprivation of life but also in cases where the person has been arrested with mischievious or malicious intention.

(II) COMPENSATORY JUSTICE IN CASES OF POLICE ATROCITIES, CUSTODIAL DEATHS AND FAKE ENCOUNTERS

Khatri v. *State of Bihar,*[11] popularly known as Bhagalpur Blinding case, was the first case where the Supreme Court considered question of jurisdiction for granting monetary compensation to the victims of police excesses. It was alleged that police blinded under trials piercing their eyes balls with needles and pouring acid in them. Mr. Justice P.N. Bhagwati speaking for the Supreme Court of India observed:

> "Why should the court not be prepared to forge new tools and devise new remedies for the purpose of indicating the most precious of the precious fundamental right to life or personal liberty."[12]

In *Arinder Singh Bagga* v. *State of U.P.,*[13] the victim Ms. Nidhi a married woman along with her husband and family members was subjected to physical, mental and psychological torture calculated to create fear to make her submit to the demands of police and abandon her legal marriage. The Supreme Court took serious view of the matter of human rights violation. The Apex Court took two dimensional decision. First, it directed to launch prosecution against concerned police officials and secondly, it directed to pay compensation of Rs. 10,000 to the victim woman and her husband and Rs. 5,000 to each other victims. The primary liability to pay compensation was fixed on the State. But it was pointed out that upon such payment, it would be open to the State of recover from the police officer concerned for the wrong done by him.

In *People's Union for Democratic Rights* v. *Police Commissioner, Delhi Police Head Quarter,*[14] Police engaged one labour for doing some work in police station. When the poor worker demanded wages, he was severely beaten and as a result of which he died. The Supreme Court awarded a sum of Rs. 75,000 as compensation to the family of the deceased worker.

Similarly in *Saheli, A Women's Resources Center* v. *Commissioner of Police*,[15] the Supreme Court again considered the question of granting compensation to the mother of the victim. A nine years old boy was taken by the police to police station. He was beaten up severely and as a consequence of beating he died. The Supreme Court awarded a compensation of Rs. 75,000 to the mother of the victim boy who died due to police assault.

Nilabati Behera v. *State of Orissa*[16] is a typical case of "custodial death." One Suman Behera, son of Nilabati Behera aged 27 years died in police custody. Suman Behera was taken from his home in police custody at about 8 A.M. on 1.12.1987 by Assistant Police Sub-Inspector Chand Darik posted at Police Station Bisara, District Sundergarh of Orissa in connection with the investigation of an offence of theft. After some time the petitioner came to know that the dead body of her son Suman Behera was found on the railway track near a bridge at some distance from the Jaraikela railway station. Several injuries were found on the body of the victim Suman Behera and his death appeared to be unnatural. The Supreme Court treated it as a 'custodial death' and awarded a sum of Rs. 1,50,000 as compensation to the mother of Suman Behera. The Court allowed compensation as a public law remedy. On the point of custodial death, Mr. Justice (as he then was) Dr. A.S. Anand observed:

> "It is an obligation of the State that there is no infringement of indefeasible rights of citizens to life, except in accordance with law while the citizen in custody. The duty of care on part of the state in strict and admits no exceptions. The wrong-doer is accountable and state is responsible if the person in custody of the police is deprived of his life except according to procedure established by the law."[17]

In *Christian Community Welfare Council of India* v. *Government of Maharashtra*,[18] the court found that the deceased Juniour Adam was done to death on account of beatings by the police personnel, an agency of sovereign power acting in violation and excess of power vested in such agency. The Court observed, "Time has come that the State Government rises to the occasion by striking the balance between the life of a person in the police custody and the power of law enforcing agencies to bring the criminals to book by appropriate rules or providing guidelines to the police personnel in such manners." The Court awarded a sum of Rs. 1,50,000 by way of compensation to the wife of the deceased.

In *Lawyers' Forum for Human Rights* v. *State of W.B.*[19] affirming the duty of State to protect the body of person in custody Calcutta High Court awarded Rs. 1,00,000 as compensation to the widow of the deceased who died in police custody.

In *Shakila Abdul Gafar Khan* v. *Vasant Raghunath Dhoble*,[20] a person died in police custody due to injuries received by him during police custody. The Supreme Court directed the State Government to pay compensation of Rs. 1,00,000 to the mother and the children of the deceased. Since, the widow got remarried, no compensation was given to her. A sum of Rs. 25,000 was given to the mother of the deceased and rest amount was paid to the children.

State liability to pay compensation has also been fixed in cases of death due to non-providing of medical assistance while in custody. Thus in *Murti Devi* v. *State of Delhi*[21] an under-trial prisoner was assaulted by some convicts in jail. After being admitted to Hospital he died due to injuries. Indicting the authorities for gross negligence the Supreme Court awarded a compensation of Rs. 2,50,000.

The Judiciary has treated the cases of non-traceable arrested persons as cases of 'custodial death' and has awarded compensation therefor. In *Sebstian M. Hongray* v. *Union of India*[22] two persons were taken into custody by army authorities at Manipur. They could not be traced. On repeated *habeas corpus*, they could not be produced before the Supreme Court. They were supposed to have met with unnatural death while in army custody. The wives of the two missing persons were awarded exemplary costs to Rs. 1,00,000 each. Similarly, in *B. Ramalamma* v. *State of A.P.*,[23] two persons had been taken into custody by the Jawans of army regiment. Later on they were reported missing. In *habeas corpus* petition by their wives the authorities detaining them could neither produce them nor could give satisfactory account for their disappearance. The Supreme Court found authorities committing contempt but instead of imposing imprisonment or fine it ordered the respondents to pay Rs. 1,00,000 to the wives of missing persons as exemplary costs in view of the torture, agony and mental oppression that they had to undergo.

In *Inder Singh* v. *State of Punjab*[24] seven persons were forcibly removed from their farm house in Majitha, district of Punjab, by a police party. On a writ petition the Supreme Court ordered the CBI to investigate the matter. The CBI report established that said seven persons were untraceable. The court, therefore, concluded that in all probability those who abducted them killed them. The Supreme Court made very appreciable observation. The Court said:

> "The primary duty of those in the uniform is to uphold law and order and protect the citizen. If members of police force resort to illegal abduction and assassination, if the members of that police force do not record and investigate complaints in this behalf for long periods of time, if those who had been abducted are found to have been unlawfully detained in police station in the state concerned prior to their probable assassination, the case is not one of errant behaviour by a member of that police force. It betrays scant respect for the life and liberty of innocent citizens and exposes the willingness of others in uniform to lend a helping hand to one who wreaks private vengeance on mere suspicion."[25]

In *Vinod Kumar* v. *State of Punjab*[26] two persons of whose disappearance was found to have been effected by the state police, were presumed to be dead. The Punjab and Haryana High Court awarded Rs. 2,00,000 to be paid as *ex gratia* to the families of the two persons who could not be searched out. In *Postsangbon N. Thokohim* v. *G.O.C.*[27] two boys were picked up by the army in Imphal on 23.9.1980. A *habeas corpus* petition was filed before the High Court. The boys could not be produced. On appeal the Supreme Court asked a report from the District Judge and report submitted to the Supreme Court concluded that there was no cogent evidence that the boys had been released. The Supreme Court directed Rs. 1,25,000 to be paid to the mothers of each of the boys. In the same vein Gauhati High Court ordered 2,00,000 to be paid to the victim's next kin in *Civil Liberties and Human Rights Organisation* v. *G.O.C.*[28] wherein a person was arrested by the Assam Rifles and his whereabout were not known for at least eight years.

The Courts have extended duty of the State to protect the life and liberty of the citizens to ensure trace of disappeared persons. In *Pushpa Gurung* v. *Asst. Director Welfare C.R.P.F.*[29] an army Jawan disappeared and authorities made no effort to trace him. The court presumed his death and ordered to pay Rs. 3,00,000 compensation for negligence in tracing out the missing Jawan.

The deplorability of custodial torture and death was very well exposed and a detailed outline to save citizens from police excesses was chalked out in *D.K. Basu* v. *State of W.B.*[30] In this case two letters from different corners sent to the Hon'ble Chief Justice of India about certain custodial deaths were treated as writ petition and were dealt with accordingly. Certain news regarding deaths in police lock ups and custody had been published in 20.7.1986, 21.7.1986 and 22.7.1986 issues of *The Telegraph* and 17.8.1986 issues of *The Statesman* and *Indian Express*. On the basis of these news the Executive Chairman of Legal Aid Services, West Bengal, a non-political organisation and registered body wrote a letter to the Chief Justice of India on 26.8.1986. He requested to treat the letter alongwith the news items as a writ petition under 'public interest litigation' category. He submitted that it was imperative to examine the issue indepth and to develop 'custody jurisprudence' and formulate modalities for awarding compensation to the victim and/or family members of the victims of atrocities and death caused in police custody and to provide for a accountability of the officers concerned.

While the matter was under consideration a letter was

written by Shri Ashok Kumar Johri on 29.7.1987 to the Chief Justice of India drawing the attention of the Hon'ble Court to the death of one Mahesh Behari of Pilkhana, Aligarh in police custody. The Supreme Court treated the letter as a writ petition and directed to list it along with the writ petition filed by Shri D.K. Basu. Keeping in view the nation-wide allegation of such incidents and news of lock-up death in all states, the Supreme Court issued notices to all the States and to the Law Commision of India for suitable suggestion. A division bench consisting of Kuldip Singh and Dr. A.S. Anand, JJ. after giving serious thought over the matter issued eleven guidelines[31] to be followed in all cases of arrest or detention till legal provisions were made in that behalf as preventive measures. The objective of directives/guidelines was to ensure effective protection of personal liberty of detenues and arrested persons. Delivering the judgment of the Court Mr. Justice (Dr.) A.S. Anand (as he then was) summed up the position regarding remedies and compensation to the victims of custodial torture. Para 54 of the judgment summing up the position runs as follow:

> "Thus, to sum up, it is now a well-accepted proposition in most of the jurisdictions, that monetary or pecuniary compensation is an appropriate and indeed an effective and sometimes perhaps the only suitable remedy for redressal of the established infringement of the fundamental right to life of a citizen by the public servants and the State is vicariously liable for their acts. The claim of the citizen is based on the principle of strict liability to which the defence of sovereign immunity is not available and the citizen must receive the amount of compensation from the State, which shall have the right to be indemnified by the wrongdoer. In the assessment of compensation, the emphasis has to be on the compensatory and not on punitive element. The objective is to apply balm to the wounds and not to punish the transgressor or the offender, as awarding appropriate punishment for the offence (irrespective of compensation) must be left to the criminal courts in which the offender is prosecuted, which the State, in

law, is duty bound to do. The award of compensation in the public law jurisdiction is also without prejudice to any other action like civil suit for damages which is lawfully available to the victim or the heirs of the deceased victim with respect to the same matter for the tortious act committed by the functionaries of the State. The quantum of compensation will, of course, depend upon the peculiar facts of each case and no strait-jacket formula can be evolved in that behalf. The relief to redress the wrong for the established invasion of the fundamental rights of the citizen, under the public law jurisdiction is, thus, in addition to the traditional remedies and not in derogation of them. The amount of compensation as awarded by the Court and paid by the State to redress the wrong done, may in a given case, he adjusted against any amount which may be awarded to the claimant by way of damages in a civil suit."

The human rights/personal liberty violation is also a serious matter in cases of encounter death. It is an extra-judicial killing and due to misuse of power by police officials, the courts interfere in such incidents and award compensation. An act of encounter is taking law into the hands by police and is a negation of rule of law. In such cases the judiciary has adopted a practical approach to the problems and has awarded compensation to the victims relatives. In *Maya Singh* v. *S.H.O., Police Station Sadar, Zira,*[32] a person was taken into custody in 1987 by the S.H.O. Sadar, Zira (Punjab). The whereabout of detenue was not known and he could not be produced before the Magistrate. It was alleged that he was killed by the Police in a police encounter in Moga Sub-division. However, there was no definite evidence that the detenue had been to eliminated. In circumstances of the case the S.H.O. was ordered to pay compensation, as an interim measure of Rs. 25,000. However, the Court left the option of reviving the issue whenever, the petitioner thought that he was sure about the fate of the detenue. In *PUCL* v. *Union of India,*[33] it was alleged that the police had killed two persons on 3.4.1991. They had been taken from Luthilian village of Manipur. An inquiry held at the behest of Supreme Court made clear that there had been no encounter as averred by the police. The Supreme Court held that "the present case appears to be one where two persons along with some others were just seized from a hut, taken a long distance away in a truck and shot there." The apex Court ordered that sum of Rs. 1,00,000 be paid to the families of each of the deceased. In *Smt. Kamini Bala Talukdar* v. *State of Assam*[34] the Gauhati High Court ordered a compensation of Rs. 1,00,000 (one lac) for cool blood killing of an active member of ULFA, a banned organisation, without making efforts to apprehend him alive. The Court gave option to authorities, if they think fit, to realize the amount from police personnel responsible for the killing of the deceased. It is submitted that the judicial outlook is laudable as it may have deterrent effect on police personnel. In *Malkiat Singh* v. *State of U.P.*,[35] the police had taken photographs of those who had been killed in an alleged encounter in Pilibhit in 1991. Talvinder Singh's photograph was identified by his father and grand father. The Supreme Court ordered a compensation of Rs. 5,00,000 (five lacs) to be paid to the victim's father.

(III) COMPENSATORY JUSTICE TO VICTIMS OF POLICE FIRING, RIOTS AND UNTOWARD HAPPENINGS

Human rights dimension of compensatory justice inspires the higher judiciary to order compensation both in cases of overaction and inaction in dealing with mob. In some cases police opens fire without any rhyme and reason and thereby violates human rights of the victims of firing. In such cases the higher judiciary comes to enforce rights of the people of life and liberty enshrined in Article 21 of the Constitution of India. Thus, in *People's Union for Democratic Rights* v. *State of Bihar*,[36] the Supreme Court awarded compensation to the victims of ruthless and unwarranted police firing. In the instant case police had opened fire without any warning at the people who were holding peaceful meeting within the compound of Gandhi Library in Arwal. The casualty due to police firing went about 21. Out of these 21 persons many children had also become victims and the several persons were injured. The Supreme Court ordered Rs. 20,000 for every case of death and Rs. 10,000 for every injured person as compensation. Delivering the judgment of the apex court Mr. Justice Rangnath Mishra observed:

> "Ordinarily in the case of death, compensation of Rs. twenty thousand is paid. We may not be taken to suggest that in case of death the liability of wrongdoer is absolved when compensation of Rs. twenty thousand is paid. But as a working principle and for convenience and with a view to rehabilitate the dependents of the deceased such compensation is paid."[37]

In *R. Gandhi* v. *Union of India,*[38] the Madras High Court came forward to compensate the victims of arson and violence following the unfortunate and distardly assassination of Prime Minister Smt. Indira Gandhi. The High Court awarded the compensation of Rs. 33,19,033 to the victims of unfortunate incident in Coimbatore. The High Court pointed out that the unfortunate victims of arson and violence are entitled to seek reasonable compensation from the State of Tamil Nadu which had failed in its duty to protect their constitutional and legal rights.

In same sequence a petition was filed in Delhi High Court to compensate the Sikh victims after the assassination of the then Prime Minister Smt. Gandhi. Several Sikhs were killed in incidence of arson and violence. Delhi High Court directed the Government of Delhi to pay a sum of Rs. 2 lakhs with interest to the aggrieved individuals. In *S.S. Ahluwalia* v. *Union of India*[39] a petition was filed in the Hon'ble Supreme Court for extension of the same benefit in view of Delhi High Court judgment to the entire country. Allowing the petition the Supreme Court observed:

> "Without examining and analyzing circumstances of each case regarding the victimization of individual it would be absolutely unwise and improper on the part of the various High Courts to grant such compensation who are not victims. Therefore, the Supreme Court

directs High Court of Delhi, Rajasthan, Orissa, Punjab and Haryana, Himachal Pradesh, Patna, Madhya Pradesh, Allahabad and Bombay to treat the petition filed in Supreme Court as a petitioned filed in the High Court and deal with the matter in respect of alimony arising in their respective jurisdiction."[40]

In *Inderpuri General Store* v. *Union of India*,[41] the High Court of Jammu and Kashmir held that State is under a constitutional obligation to compensate the victim adequately as the State failed to protect the life, liberty and property of the citizens in the communal riots.

The judicial trend is welcome. The Supreme Court has played an appreciable role in this regard. It has compensated the victims of unwarranted firing and communal riots or riots due to certain special incidence of violence. It is a healthy trend in direction of ensuring justice to the victims of riot or other untoward happenings by fixing responsibility to compensate on state for its failure to ensure protection of life and liberty of the citizens. Thus in *MCD* v. *Association of the victims of Uphaar Tragedy*[42] wherein a cinema Hall caught fire and tragedy cost many lives. The High Court granted compensation to the victims as follows:

(A) Compensation awarded to the deceased below the age group of 20 yrs. (No. of deceased 23) Rs.15,00,000	Rs. 3,45,00,000
(B) Compensation awarded to the deceased above the age of group of 20 yrs. (No. of deceased 36) Rs.18,00,000	Rs. 6,48,00,000
(C) Compensation awarded to the injured (No. of injured 103) Rs.1,00,000	Rs. 1.03,00,000
Total principal amount awarded (A+B+C)	Rs. 10,96,00,000
55% of the principal amount payable by Ansal Theatre and Clubotels (P) Ltd.	Rs. 6,02,80,000
50% of the principal amount	Rs. 3,01,40,000

The Supreme Court affirmed the stand of the High Court. Again in *Chief Secretary* v. *Students of A.P.A.U.*[43] an unfortunate incident took place on 13.9.1996 in which one Srinivas Reddy (since deceased) threw acid on Ms Anuradha, a B.Sc. (Ag.) final year student, causing extensive burn injuries to her. The students of the University sent a letter/ petition to the High Court of Andhra Pradesh, which was treated as public interest petition and was numbered as WP No. 19820 of 1996. The High Court ordered payment of Rs. 5 lakhs (Rs. 5,00,000) to the Victim Ms Anuradha and issued four directions. The directions ran as follow:

"(1) The State of Andhra Pradesh shall provide to the second petitioner Ms Anuradha full and complete treatment for the burn injuries suffered by her, including surgery and plastic surgery for repair of the damages, in particular, including all costs and expenses on treatment, hospitalisation and transport, etc. In course of the treatment and for all the above, give exclusive expert treatment in the government hospitals as well as in other hospitals where best treatment for the wounds suffered by her is available. The State shall meet all expenses of her lodging and board in hospitals and/or nursing homes and/or any other place where she is permitted to stay by the attending physicians/surgeons.

(2) The University shall permit the second petitioner to appear in the examinations without her complying with the necessary conditions of attendance of classes, etc., and make such arrangements for her writing the examinations which attending physicians/surgeons would recommend. On her completing the studies, if any further she would desire to study; the University would admit her to the course/courses of study of her choice without insisting for any entrance examination and/or fulfilment of the merit for the purpose of selection, etc. In case, on the basis of her qualifications already acquired, she decides to go for a job or service and befitting her qualifications there is any job in the University,

the University shall give to her the job and shall, for the said purpose, relax all conditions of recruitment.

(3) The State Government shall appoint a Special Prosecutor and entrust the case to him for prosecuting N. Srinivas Reddy and ensure that Ms Anuradha and other witnesses are provided full protection and are given necessary batta, etc., on time as and when they are required to depose in the case.

(4) The University shall issue necessary notification/ order with respect to the appointment of a retired Judge of the High Court duly nominated by the Chief Justice for enquiry into the allegations against the Principal—the second respondent and other persons who have allegedly indulged in misconducts as per the statements in the report of Smt. Annapurna Devi, Advocate. The enquiry in this behalf shall be completed within a period of two months."

On appeal the Supreme Court affirmed the order of High Court. Since, meanwhile, the Chief Minister had granted *ex gratia* payment of Rs. 2,00,000 (two lakhs) to Ms Anuradha, that amount was ordered to be adjusted within the amount of Rs. 5,00,000.

(IV) COMPENSATORY JUSTICE TO THE VICTIMS OF RAPE

In January, 1990 the Supreme Court directed the Government of Bihar to pay compensation to a rape victim. An Eighteen year old tribal girl was allegedly raped by the police. The Supreme Court ordered a sum of Rs. 50,000 to be paid to the rape victim by the State.[44] In another case the Supreme Court directed Punjab Government to make payment of Rs. 15,000 to each of the relatives of the victim of the rape. In this case two minor girls had been allegedly kidnapped, raped and killed by police officials.[45]

There is a triology of the Supreme Court decisions

which marks a revolutionary progress in the field of compensatory justice to the victims of rape. In *Delhi Domestic Working Women's Forum* v. *Union of India*[46] a public interest litigation was filed by Delhi Domestic Working Women's Forum under Article 32 of the Constitution to espouse the pathetic plight of domestic servants who were subjected to indecent assault by army personnel in a train. Taking note of the seriousness of the matter, the Supreme Court of India evolved the power to award interim compensation and issued a number of guidelines in assisting the victims of rape. The Supreme Court Division Bench consisting of Kuldeep Singh and S. Saghir Ahmad, JJ. observed that:

> "If the Court trying an offence of rape has jurisdiction to award the compensation at the final stage, there is no reason to deny to the Court the right to award interim compensation. The jurisdiction of the courts trying the offence of rape which is an offence against the basic human rights and also fundamental right of personal life and liberty. Unfortunately a woman in our country, belongs to a class of group of society who are in a disadvantaged position on account of several social barriers and impediments and have, therefore, been the victim of tyranny at the hands of men with whom they fortunately under Constitution enjoy equal rights."

The idea of interim compensation to rape-victims is quite innovative and welcome. In addition to it the Supreme Court chalked out a broad scheme for legal and financial assistance to the victims of rape. The scheme and suggestions indicated by the Supreme Court is worth-noting:

> "In this background, it is necessary to indicate the broad parameters in assisting the victims of rape:"

(1) The complainants of sexual assault cases should be provided with legal representation. It is important to have someone who is well-acquainted with the criminal justice system. The role of the victim's advocate would not only be to explain to the

victim the nature of the proceedings, to prepare her for the case and to assist her in the police station and in court but to provide her with guidance as to how she might obtain help of a different nature from other agencies, for example, mind counselling or medical assistance. It is important to secure continuity of assistance by ensuring that the same person who looked after the complainant's interests in the police station represent her till the end of the case.

(2) Legal assistance will have to be provided at the police station since the victim of sexual assault might very well be in a distressed state upon arrival at the police station, the guidance and support of a lawyer at this stage and whilst she was being questioned would be of great assistance to her.

(3) The police should be under a duty to inform the victim of her right to representation before any questions were asked of her and that the police report should state that the victim was so informed.

(4) A list of advocates willing to act in these cases should be kept at the police station for victims who did not have a particular lawyer in mind or whose own lawyer was unavailable.

(5) The Advocate shall be appointed by the court, upon application by the police at the earliest convenient moment, but in order to ensure that victims were questioned without undue delay, advocates would be authorised to act at the police station before leave of the court was sought or obtained.

(6) In all rape trials anonymity of the victim must be maintained, as far as necessary.

(7) It is necessary, having regard to the Directive Principles contained under Article 38(1) of the Constitution of India to set-up Criminal Injuries Compensation Board. Rape victims frequently incur substantial financial loss. Some, for example, are too traumatised to continue in employment.

(8) Compensation for victims shall be awarded by the court on conviction of the offender and by the Criminal Injuries Compensation Board whether or not a conviction has taken place. The Board will take into account pain, suffering and shock as well as loss of earnings due to pregnancy and the expenses of child birth if this occurred as a result of the rape.[47]

It is submitted that the observation of the Supreme Court as to legal assistance and other parameters assisting the rape victim is most welcome. The suggestion to constitute Criminal Injuries Compensation Board to assist rape victims is sound. The suggestion of Court to payment of compensation by offender in cases of conviction and in other cases where prosecution does not culminate in conviction, by Criminal Injuries Board is quite appreciable and is in tune with security measures prevailing in western countries. The suggestion as to maintenance expenditure to pregnancy caused by the alleged rape should be taken into note while awarding compensation shows the willingness and consciousness of the court to safeguard the interest of rape victims.

The public law remedy in relation to the victims of rape was extended to the private cases of rape in *Bodhisattva Gautam* v. *Subhra Chakraborty*.[48] In this case Subhra, a student of the Bapist College of Kohima filed a complaint against Bodhisattva Gautam, a lecturer in the same college that he used to visit her residence and induced her to cohabit with him by giving a false assurance of marriage. He had also undergone through fake marriage ceremony. He compelled her to undergo abortion twice against her will. In appeal to the Supreme Court against the order of the High Court rejecting his application to quash criminal proceedings initiated against him by Subhra, the Supreme Court not only dismissed his appeal but also issued *suo motu* notice to Bodhisatva calling upon him to show why he should not be asked to pay compensation for maintenance of Subhra Chakraborty during the pendency of the prosecution against him. The Supreme Court ordered payment of a sum of

Rs. 1000 per month to Subhra during the pendency of the criminal proceeding. It also directed Bodhisatva Gautam to pay arrears of compensation at the same rate from the date on which the complaint was filed till date. The Supreme Court made certain very valuable observations of far-reaching consequences. It pointed out that rape (and other sexual infraction of the person) amounts to violation of most cherished right to life and dignity as guaranteed under Article 21 of the Constitution. The court reiterated the proposal of setting up of Criminal Injuries Compensation Board (as was suggested in Delhi Domestic Working Women's Forum case).

The most revolutionary and valuable contribution of the Supreme Court in *Bodhisattva Gautam's* case is the assertion of its power to award interim compensation even against private bodies or individuals in exercise of its writ jurisdiction. It is submitted that the court introduced a new concept of public low remedy holding an individual liable for violating Article 21 and holding such cases amenable to writ jurisdiction. Thus, in rape cases fundamental rights can be enforced not only against state but also against private individuals by (i) writ court *suo motu* or (ii) through Public interest litigation or (iii) by victims.

The Supreme Court has glorified and extended the area of compensatory justice to the victims of rape by acknowledging that the protection against rape and other sexual infractions of the person as guaranteed Article 21 is available to all—be the victim Indian national or a foreigner. This judicial stand of the Supreme Court was indicated in *Chairman, Railway Board and others* v. *Mrs. Chandrima Das.*[49] In this case a foreign national, Bangladeshi woman Smt. Hanuffa Khatoon was gang raped by railway employees of Eastern Railway in a room at Yatri Niwas of Howrah Station of Eastern Railway. Mrs. Chandrima Das, a practising advocate of the Calcutta High Court filed a writ petition under Article 226 of the Constitution against the various railway authorities of Eastern Railway claiming compensation for the victim. The High Court had awarded a sum of Rs. 10,00,000 (ten lakhs) as compensation to Smt. Hanuffa Khatoon. The Supreme Court of India appreciating the order of the Calcutta High Court observed:

> "Smt. Hanuffa Khatoon was entitled to be treated with dignity and was entitled to the protection of her person as guaranteed under Article 21 of the Constitution. As a national of another country, she could not be subjected to a treatment which was below dignity, nor could she be subjected to physical violence at the hands of Government employees who outraged her modesty. The right available to her under Article 21 was thus violated consequently; the state was under the constitutional liability to pay compensation to her. The judgment passed by the Calcutta High Court, therefore, allowing compensation to her having been gang raped cannot be said to suffer any infirmity."

The highest court of the land has played very laudable and creative role in awarding compensation with a view to ensure justice to a woman even in the case the accused was not convicted. In *Deelip Singh* v. *State of Bihar,*[50] the appellant by promising to marry the victim woman persuaded her to have sexual relations and caused pregnancy. Though he was not convicted under section 376 of the I.P.C., the court awarded a compensation of Rs. 50,000 as monetary compensation irrespective of his acquittal. It was done so by the court under Article 142, the Constitution of India with a view to render complete justice.

It is submitted that Judiciary, more particularly the higher Judiciary, has played very laudable role in awarding compensation to the victims of crime through the new way of public law remedy. It has reinforced the idea that the State has duty to protect life, liberty and property of the people. In cases of any failure on the part of the State to ensure such security, it is duty of the state to compensate the victims which they can claim as a matter of right or entitlement and is no more a matter of governmental grace.

The study of the present chapter is clear indicator of state liability to provide compensation to the victims of illegal arrest and unwarranted detention; police atrocities, custodial death and fake encounters; police firing, riots and untoward happenings and rape. The courts have played very significant role in awarding compensation by doing away with a line of distinction between the private remedy against individuals and the public remedy against the State. Thus, individuals have also been treated amenable unit jurisdiction for enforcement of right to life and personal liberty. It can be done by the writ court *suo motu* or through public interest petition or on initiative compensation. They have extended the protection of life and liberty to a victim who is not Indian national but a foreigner. The courts have also made valuable suggestions regarding the setting up of Criminal Injuries Compensation Board with a view to award compensation to victims where prosecution of accused do not culminate in conviction. Last but not the least, Judiciary has suggested a number of assistance measures to be provided to the victims so as to give a healing touch and enable them to cooperate actively in administration of justice.

Notes and References

1. Merryman, John Henry, *The Civil Law Tradition* (1969), p. 132.
2. Culhane, California Enacts Legislation to Aid Victims of Criminal Violence, 18, *Stanford Law Review* (1965) 262 at p. 272.
3. Sube Singh *v.* State of Haryana (2006) 3 S.C.C. 178 at p. 199 (Ravindran J. speaking for a three judge bench).
4. Bodhisattva Gautam *v.* Subhra Chakraborty, A.I.R. 1996 S.C. 922;
5. A.I.R. 1983 S.C. 1086.
6. *Ibid.*
7. (Unreported) quoted in M.P. Jain and S.N. Jain, *Principles of Administrative Law* (1986), p. 781.
8. (1991) Cr.L.J. 1680 (Med.). See also Natim Bhanot *v.* Commissioner of Police, A.I.R. 1990 A.C.T. 345 (S.C.).
9. A.I.R. 1986 S.C. 494.
10. *Ibid.*
11. A.I.R. 1982 S.C. 928.
12. *Ibid.* at p. 930.
13. A.I.R. 1984 S.C. 571.
14. (1989) 4 S.C.C. 730.
15. A.I.R. 1990 S.C. 513.
16. A.I.R. 1993 S.C. 1960.
17. *Ibid.*
18. (1994) Mah. L.J. 1769.

19. (1997) 1 Cal. N.C.N. 485.
20. (2003) 7 S.C.C. 749.
21. (1998) 9 S.C.C. 604.
22. A.I.R. 1979 S.C. 1026.
23. (1993) 1 Scale 90.
24. A.I.R. 1995 S.C. 1949.
25. *Ibid.*, p. 1951.
26. (1996) Cr.L.J. 1037 (P. and H.).
27. (1997) 7 S.C.C. 725.
28. (1997) 1 Gau. L.T. 91.
29. (1988) 86 Cutt. L.T. 319.
30. (1997) 1 S.C.C. 416.
31. The Supreme Court issued the following guidelines to be followed in all cases of arrest or detention till legal provisions are made in that behalf as preventive measures:

(1) "The police personnel carrying out the arrest and handling the interrogation of the arrestee should bear accurate, visible and clear identification and name tags with their designations. The particulars of all such police personnel who handle interrogation of the arrestee must be recorded in a register.

(2) That the police officer carrying out the arrest of the arrestee shall prepare a memo of arrest at the time of arrest and such memo shall be attested by at least one witness, who may either be a member of the family of the arrestee or a respectable person of the locality from where the arrest is made. It shall also be countersigned by the arrestee and shall contain the time and date of arrest.

(3) A person who has been arrested or detained and is being held in custody in a police station or interrogation centre of other lock-up, shall be entitled to have one friend or relative or other person known to him or having interest in his welfare being informed, as soon as practicable, that he has been arrested and is being detained at the particular place, unless the attesting witness of the memo of arrest is himself such a friend or a relative of the arrestee.

(4) The time, place of arrest and venue of custody of an arrestee must be notified by the police where the next friend or relative of the arrestee lives outside the district or town through the Legal Aid Organisation in the District and the police state of the area concerned telegraphically within a period of 8 to 12 hours after the arrest.

(5) The person arrested must be made aware of this right to have someone informed of his arrest or detention as soon as he is put under arrest or is detained.

(6) An entry must be made in the diary at the place of detention regarding the arrest of the person which shall also disclose the name of the next friend of the person who has been informed of the arrest and the names and particulars of the police officials in whose custody the arrestee is.

(7) The arrestee should, where he so requests, be also examined at the time of his arrest and major and minor injuries, if any present on his/her body, must be recorded at that time. The "Inspection Memo" must be signed both by the arrestee and the police officer effecting the arrest and its copy provided to the arrestee.

(8) The arrestee should be subjected to medical examination by a trained doctor every 48 hours during his detention in custody by a doctor on the panel of approved doctors appointed by Director, Health Services of the State or Union Territory concerned. Director, Health Services should prepare such a panel for all tehsils and districts as well.

(9) Copies of all the documents including the memo of arrest, referred to above, should be sent to the Illaqa Magistrate for his record.

(10) The arrestee may be permitted to meet his lawyer during interrogation, though not throughout the interrogation.

(11) A police control room should be provided at all district and State headquarters, where information regarding the arrest and the place of custody of the arrestee shall be communicated by the officer causing the arrest, within 12 hours of effecting the arrest and at the police control room it should be displayed on a conspicuous notice board.

32. (1991) A.C.J. 439 (P. and H.)
33. (1997) 3 S.C.C. 433.
34. (1997) Cr.L.J. 874 (Gau.).
35. (1998) 9S.C.C. 351.
36. A.I.R. 1987 S.C. 355.
37. *Ibid.* at p. 356.
38. A.I.R. 1989 Mad. 205.
39. A.I.R. 2001 S.C. 1309.
40. *Ibid.*
41. A.I.R. 1992 J. and K. 2.
42. (2005) 9S.C.C. 586.
43. (2005) 12 S.C.C. 448.
44. *Legal News and Views,* 47, Reprinted in XXVIII *Annual Survey of Indian Law* (1990), p. 32.
45. *The Hindustan Times*, 26 April, 1990, Reprinted in XXVIII *ASIL* (1990), p. 32.
46. (1995) 1 S.C.C. 14.
47. *Ibid.*
48. A.I.R. 1996 S.C. 922.
49. A.I.R. 2000 S.C. 988.
50. A.I.R. 2005 S.C. 203.

7

Epilogue

Justice to all is the call of all the civilized nations. Justice as fairness is due to all components of the administration of criminal justice. Victims of crime once thought as neglected and 'forgotten men' have attracted concern of the civilized society as an important segment.

The study shows that in historical perspective victims are reaching towards regaining their position what was secured in early times of administration of justice when there was no clear cut dividing line between the civil and criminal justice administration process. But, it had seen many ups and down. In historical process the victim's place was taken by the state and he got ignored in the process. But by and by victim's role got resurrection. The claim of victim for restitution and compensation was recognised. The study also establishes that with the change of the concept of state, i.e. change from *laissez-faire* to welfare state and changing dimension of justice, the criminal justice system experienced a shift from punitive justice to the restorative justice. This shift invited the victim's claim for compensatory justice as well as assistance. The study also shows a world-wide trend towards the realization of victim's rights. The meaning of victim became very liberal and wide especially in view of the United Nations Declaration of Basic Principles of Justice for

Victims and Abuse of Power. Restitution, compensation and assistance were recognized as form of the help for the victims of crime. Both civil law countries like France, Germany and other continental countries and common law countries like United Kingdom and U.S.A. adopted a number of progressive measures of compensatory justice with a view to provide respectability and justice to the victims of crime. The study also shows different measures of restitutive and compensatory or assistance schemes applicable to victims in India. But the position of administration of criminal justice in India has not been very encouraging due to discretionary nature of the compensatory orders and suspicion about the realization of fines imposed on offenders.

The main hypothesis that despite some efforts—statutory and judicial, the provisions ensuring justice to victims and thereby inspiring their active role in criminal justice system, India has not achieved its intended goals and much is needed to keep Indian pace with victim-oriented justice on par with the measures adopted elsewhere in the world has been approved and established in view of the study of comparative position in countries of civil law traditions and common law traditions except India. Even in common law countries like United States of America and the United Kingdom the measures adopted to ensure justice to the victims of crime have been more progressive and practical in view of involvement of public funds. India lags behind in this respect. Indian adversial/accusatorial system still is more and more favourable to the accused/offenders and victims of crime remain neglected. Though some rules framed under S.C.s and S.T.s (Prevention of Atrocities) Act, 1989 have given some sorts of monetary assistance and compensation to the victims but in many more cases there is paucity or absence of statutory provisions. In some cases judiciary has taken lead and issued guidelines, e.g. in rape cases and in cases of custodial treatments but legislature does not appear to be much enthusiastic in safeguarding the position of victims. Thus, the study reveals that in India judiciary, especially during last three decades has been very progressive in dealing with the problems of victims of crime and it has shown its sensitiveness as well. It is clear from the observation of Mr. Justice V.R. Krishna Iyer in *Rattan Singh v. State of Punjab*[1] wherein the learned judge pointed out, "It is a weakness of our jurisprudence that victim of crime and the distress of the dependants of the victim do not attract the attention of law . . . This is the deficiency in the system which must be rectified." In *Harikishan* v. *Sukhbir Singh*[2] the Supreme Court commented that section 357, Cr.P.C. has not been used properly. It said that the courts have seldom involved this power due to the ignorance of the object of it. The insufficiency of section 357, Cr.P.C. has also been exposed by the Law Commission of India which lamented that courts do not exercise their salutary power as freely and liberally as they could be desired.[3]

Of course, the study established that judiciary has played very laudable and progressive role in providing compensation to the victims of illegal arrest and unwarranted detentions, police atrocities, custodial deaths and fake encounters; police firing, riots and untoward happenings, rape, etc. It has evolved the concept of public law remedy in such cases. It has done away or at least minimised the public and private remedy distinction in the area of violation of personal liberty and life guaranteed under Article 21 of the Constitution of India. Even individuals have been held amenable to writ jurisdiction under Articles 32 and 226 of the Constitution of India. But the judiciary has its own limitations. It gets mobilized only when cases come to it. *Secondly*, judicial outlook may differ from case to case. To make it more clear the progressive and victim-oriented judgment of the Supreme Court in *Harikishan* v. *Sukhbir Singh*[4] to compensate the victim of crime under Section 357(3) of the Cr.P.C. was not followed in two of its latter cases, *Brij Lal* v. *Prem Chand*[5] and *State of U.P.* v. *Jodh Singh*.[6] Similarly, the Supreme Courts' approach to award compensation and interim maintenance in *Bodhisattva Gautam's case*[7] did not continue in *A.K. Singh* v. *Uttrakhand Jan Morcha*,[8] wherein the Supreme Court set aside the compensation awarded by the High Court for molestation in a public interest petition pending prosecution, but granted liberty to aggrieved the person to approach the competent court for compensation and in *Mukeshbhai Nanubhai Patil* v. *State of Gujarat*,[9] the

Gujarat High Court confined the *Bodhisattva Gautam's* case[10] to the facts of that case and set aside the order granting interim relief pending trial.

In India the victims of the crimes still remain "forgotten men" in the criminal justice system. As a whole, system of administration of justice ignores victims' interest and often treats them unfairly. There are elaborate and extensive procedural rights of the accused but victims' interests are ignored more than often. There is urgent necessity to enhance the rights and privileges of crime victims because it will encourage victims' participation in the criminal justice system and ensure successfulness of investigation and prosecution. The need of hour in the country is to do away with inequity between a fully articulated system of procedural rights of the accused and the virtually non-existent procedural rights of the victims. With a view to encourage the victims to play their active and fruitful role and ensure justice to them a number of statutory changes are needed.

SUGGESTIONS

Due to ineffectiveness and inadequacy of provisions ensuring justice to the victims of crime a number of substantive and procedural safeguards are needed along with assistance schemes and public fund to compensate the victims of crime in light of the recommendation of Commission, Committees and judicial directions issued from time to time. The following suggestions are proffered with a view to ensure justice to the victims and encourage their participation in the criminal justice system.

1. The Indian Penal Code should be appropriately amended as to provide a substantive provision for payment of compensation as one of the modes of punishment. Such an amendment is long over due in view of the Law Commission of India 42nd Report and Indian Penal Code (Amendment) Bill, 1972 which could not materialise.

With a view to fulfil the requirement of the end of justice to the poorer section of the people where accused is in a position to amends, section 53 of the Indian Penal Code should be amended so as to read as follows:

53. The punishment to which offenders are liable under the provisions of this code are—
First—Death.
Secondly—Imprisonment for life.
Thirdly—(Repealed by Act No. XVII of 1949).
Fourthly—Imprisonment, which is of two descriptions, namely:
(1) Rigorous, that is, with hard labour, and
(2) Simple.
Fifthly—Forfeiture of property;
Sixthly—Fine;
Seventhly—Payment of compensation.

2. It is suggested that victims of the crime should be kept on par with the accused. As sections 235(2) and 248(2) of Cr.P.C. provide for opportunity to the accused of being heard on the question of sentence, there should be provision to ensure victim being heard before passing of sentence. Thus a new section should be added after section 357 of the Cr.P.C., 1973 as follows:
Section 357-A: In the case the accused is convicted for an offence charged against person, property and the reputation, the victim will be given an opportunity of being heard on loss or injury caused to him due to offence and thereafter the court will pass the sentence on the accused according to law.

3. *Section 357(3) be substituted by the following new clause:*
S. 357(3): When a court imposes a sentence of which fine does not form a part, the court shall, while passing the judgment, order the accused person to pay, by way of compensation, such amount as may be specified in the order to the victim who has suffered any loss or injury by the

reason of the act for which the accused person has been so sentenced:

Provided that if the accused is not in a position to financially make amends to the victim, victim or his dependents as the case may be will be compensated out of earnings of the accused while earning in prison by doing work:

Provided further that if the court chooses not to order the accused to pay the victim by way of compensation any amount, the court shall record reasons for not doing so.

4. Since compensation is awarded by the court only on conviction of the offender, it is suggested that a Criminal Injuries Compensation Board should be set-up. The Board will award compensation whether or not a conviction has taken place. More particularly in the cases of rape or other sexual exploitations/violence the Board will have to take into account pains, suffering and shock as well as loss of earnings due to pregnancy and expenses of child birth if this occurred as a result of rape.
5. Since State has duty to protect the life, liberty and property of the citizens state should constitute a victim compensation fund to compensate the victim, more particularly to:
   (i) Victims of terrorism;
   (ii) Victims of environmental offences;
   (iii) Victims of violence, riots, communal violence, political violence, violence by naxalites and other violence claiming mass lives and suffering;
   (iv) Victims of rape and other sexual offences;
   (v) Victims of abuse of power by public officials;
   (vi) Victims of Law and order failure;
   (vii) Victims of domestic violence;
   (viii) Sexually Exploited and other Abused Children; and
   (ix) Victims of Telemarketing fraud.
6. State should take responsibility to compensate the victims, more particularly:

(a) where offender is unknown and unidentified and cannot be apprehended.
(b) when offender is not convicted of the alleged offence;
(c) where offender is unable to compensate; and
(d) where offender makes amend to victim but compensation is not adequate.

7. Criminal justice system should be made more humane to the victims. Police officials should be made more and more liable for custodial excesses. On the line of the 133rd Report of the Law Commission of India, Evidence Act, 1872 should be appropriately amended so as to provide presumption as to injuries caused in police custody that injuries were caused by the police officer under whose custody the victim was kept. Furthermore, Section 197 of the Code of Criminal Procedure, 1973 providing for sanction of the State to prosecute certain police officers should be qualified by a proviso like follow:
"Provided that nothing contained in this section shall apply in case of custodial offences where the Court on an inquiry is *prima-facie* of the opinion that the accused public servant committed an offence of penal nature within his custody."
8. Statutory provisions should make the criminal justice system to operate for victims. Victims should not feel ignored. He should be kept in mainstream of the administration of justice process. They should be treated affectionately; informed of their rights, be provided legal assistance, their privacy be protected; minimum inconvenience be caused to them; proper security be provided to victim/witnesses; undue delay be avoided and expenses incurred by them in co-operating prosecution be reimbursed.
9. Social and voluntary organisations should be encouraged to take up victim assistance programmes seriously for providing assistances and supports to victims and thereby arousing a sense of security among them.

Last but not the least; the legislative inaction should be given goodbye. It is a welcome move that the government is going to add section 357(A) and allowing victim to right to appeal and providing stern action against falls F.I.Rs. However, much is needed. The legislature should march alongwith Report of the Commission, Committees and Victimological researches done as well as the judicial sensitiveness expressed in a number of cases dealing with female workers, rape-victims, custodial torture and so on so forth. Should not our Parliament and State Legislatures be ready to play active part in 21st century to ensure justice to victims (expanding in range now) of crime on line with international norms, commissions' report and judicial awakenings and ensure meaningful application of our constitutional commitment to ensure justice to all including the victims?

Notes and References

1. (1997) 4 S.C.C. 719.
2. A.I.R. 1988 S.C. 2127.
3. The Law Commission of India, Forty-first Report: The Code of Criminal Procedure, Vol. I (1969), p. 366.
4. A.I.R. 1988 S.C. 2127.
5. A.I.R. 1989 S.C. 1661.
6. A.I.R. 1989 S.C. 1822.
7. A.I.R. 1996 S.C. 922.
8. A.I.R. 1999 S.C. 2193.
9. 1998 Cr.L.J. 194.
10. A.I.R. 1996 S.C. 922.

APPENDIX

UN DECLARATION OF BASIC PRINCIPLES OF JUSTICE FOR VICTIMS OF CRIME AND ABUSE OF POWER

(A) GENERAL ASSEMBLY RESOLUTION

General Assembly Resolution 40/34

The General Assembly

Recalling that the Sixtieth United Nations Congress on the Prevention of Crime and the Treatment of offenders that the United Nations should continue its present work on the development of guidelines and standards regarding abuse of economic and political power.

Cognizant that millions of people throughout the world suffer harm as a result of crime and the abuse of power and that the rights of these victims have not been adequately recognized.

Recognizing that the victims of crime and the victims of abuse of power, and also frequently their families, witnesses and others who aid them, are unjustly subjected to loss, damage or injury and that they may, in addition, suffer hardship when assisting in the prosecution of offender,

(1) Affirms the necessity of adopting national and international measures in order to secure the universal and effective recognition of, and respect for, the rights of victims of crime and of abuse of power;

(2) Stresses the need to promote progress by all States in their efforts to that end, without prejudice to the rights of suspects or offenders;

(3) Adopts the Declaration of Basic Principles of Justice for Victims of Crime and Abuse of Power, annexed to the present resolution, which is designed to assist Governments and the International community in their efforts to secure justice and assistance for victims of crime and victims of abuse of power;

(4) Calls upon Member States to take the necessary steps to give efforts to the provisions contained in the Declaration and, in order to curtail victimization as referred to hereinafter, endeavour—

(i) To implement socials health, including mental health, educational economic and specific crime prevention policies to reduce victimization and encourage assistance to victims in distress;

(ii) To promote community efforts and public participation in crime prevention;

(iii) To review periodically their existing legislation and practice in order to ensure responsiveness to changing circumstances, and to enact and enforce legislation proscribing acts that violate internationally recognized norms relating to human rights, corporate conduct, and other abuses of power;

(iv) To establish and strengthen the means of detecting, prosecuting and sentencing those guilty of crimes;

(v) To promote disclosure of relevant information to expose official; and corporate conduct to public scrutiny and other ways of increasing responsiveness to public concerns;

(vi) To promote the observance of codes of conduct and ethical norms, in a particular international standards, by public servants, including law enforcement, correctional, medical, social service and military personnel as well as the staff of economic enterprises;

(vii) To prohibit practices and procedures

conductive to abuse, such as secret places of detention and incommunicado detention; and

(viii) To co-operate with other States, through mutual judicial and administrative assistance, in such matters as the detection and pursuit of offenders, their extradition and the seizure of their assets, to be used for restitution to the victims;

(5) Recommends that, at the international and regional levels, all appropriate measures should be taken:

(i) To promote training activities designed to foster adherence to United Nations Standards and norms and to curtail possible abuses;

(ii) To sponsor collaborative action-research on ways in which victimization can be reduced and victims aided, and to promote information exchanges, on the most effective means of so doing;

(iii) To render direct aid, to requesting governments designed to help them curtail victimization and alleviate the plight of victims; and

(iv) To develop ways and means of providing recourse for victims where national channels may be insufficient;

(6) Requests the Secretary-General to invite Member-States to report periodically to the General Assembly on the implementation of the Declaration, as well as on measures taken by them to this effect.

(7) Also requests the Secretary-General to make use of the opportunities, which all relevant bodies and organizations within the United Nations system offer to assist Member-States, whenever necessary, in improving ways and means of protecting victims both at the national level and through international cooperation;

(8) Further requests the Secretary-General to promote the objectives of the Declaration, in particular by ensuring its widest possible dissemination;

(9) Drugs the specialized agencies and other entities and bodies of the United Nations system, other relevant inter-governmental and non-governmental organizations and the public to co-operate in the implementation of the provisions of the Declaration.

(B) UN DECLARATION OF BASIC PRINCIPLES OF JUSTICE FOR VICTIMS OF CRIME AND ABUSE OF POWER

(a) Victims of Crime

(1) Victims means who, individually or collectively, have suffered harm, including physical or mental injury, emotional suffering, economic loss or substantial impairment of their fundamental rights, through acts or omission that are in violation of criminal laws operative within Member-States, including those laws proscribing criminal abuse of power.

(2) A person may be considered a victim, under this Declaration, regardless of whether the perpetrator is identified, apprehended, prosecuted or convicted and regardless of the familiar relationship between the perpetrator and the victim. The term victim also includes, where appropriate, the immediate family or dependants of the direct victim and persons who have suffered harm in intervening to assist victims in distress or to prevent victimization.

(3) The provisions contained herein shall be applicable to all, without distinction of any kind, such as race, colour, sex, age, language, religion, nationality, political or other opinion, cultural beliefs or practices, property, birth or family status, ethnic or social origin, and disability.

Access to justice and fair treatment

(4) Victims should be treated with compassion and

respect for their dignity. They are entitled to access to the mechanisms of justice and to prompt redress, as provided for by national legislation, for the harm that they have suffered.

(5) Judicial and administrative mechanisms should be established and strengthened where necessary to enable victims to obtain redress through formal or informal procedures that are expeditious, fair inexpensive and accessible. Victims should be informed to their rights in seeking redress through such mechanisms.

(6) The responsiveness of judicial and administrative processes to the needs of victims should be facilitated by:

(i) Informing victims of their role and the scope, timing and progress of the proceeding and of the disposition of their cases, especially where serious crimes are involved and where they have requested such information;

(ii) Allowing the views and concerns of victims to be presented and considered at appropriate stages of the proceedings where their personal interests are affected, without prejudice to the accused and consistent with the relevant national criminal justice system;

(iii) Providing proper assistance to victims through the legal process;

(iv) Taking measures to minimize inconvenience of victims, protect their safety, as well as that of their families and witnesses on their behalf, from intimidation and retaliation; and

(v) Avoiding unnecessary delay in the disposition of cases and the execution of orders or decrees granting awards to victims.

(7) Informal mechanisms for the resolution of disputes, including mediation, arbitration and customary justice or indigenous practice, should be utilized where appropriate to facilitate conciliation and redress for victims.

Restitution

(8) Offenders or third parties responsible for their behavior should, where appropriate, make fair restitution to victims, their families or dependants. Such restitution should include the return or property or payment for the harm or loss suffered reimbursement of expenses of services and the restoration of rights.

(9) Governments should review their practices, regulations and laws to consider restitution as an available sentencing option in criminal cases, in addition to other criminal sanctions.

(10) In cases of substantial harm to the environment, restitution, if ordered, should include, as far as possible, restoration of the environment, reconstruction of the infrastructure, replacement of community facilities and reimbursement of the expenses of relocation, wherever such harm results in the dislocation of a community.

(11) Where public officials or other agents acting in an official or quasi-official capacity have violated national criminal laws, the victims should receive restitution from the State whose officials or agents were responsible for the Government under whose authority the victimizing act or omission occurred is no longer in existence, the State of Government successor in title should provide restitution to the victims.

Compensation

(12) When compensation is not fully available from the offender or other sources, States should endeavour to provide financial compensation to:

(a) Victims who have sustained significant bodily injury or impairment of physical or mental health as a result of serious crimes;

(b) The family, in particular dependants of persons who have died or become physically or mentally incapacitated as a result of such victimization.

(13) The establishment, strengthening and expansion of

national funds for compensation to victims should be encouraged. Where appropriate, other funds may also be established for the purpose, including those cases where the State of which the victim is a national is not in a position to compensate the victim for the harm.

Assistance

(14) Victims should receive the necessary material, medical, psychological and social assistance through government, voluntary, community-based and indigenous means.

(15) Victims should be informed of the availability of health and social services and other relevant assistance and be readily afforded access to them.

(16) Police, justice, health, social service and other personnel concerned should received training to sensitize them to the needs of victims, and guidelines to ensure proper and prompt aid.

(17) In providing services and assistance to victims, attention should be given to those who have special needs because of the nature of the harm inflicted or because of factors such as those, mentioned in paragraph 3 above.

(b) Victims of abuse of power

(18) Victims means persons who, individually or collectively, have suffered harm, including physical or mental injury, emotional suffering, economic loss or substantial impairment of their fundamental rights, through acts or omissions that do not yet constitute violations of national criminal laws but of internationally recognized norms relating to human rights.

(19) States should consider incorporating into the national law norms proscribing abuses of power and providing remedies to victims of such abuses. In particular, such remedies should include restitution and/or compensation, and social assistance and support.

(20) States should consider negotiating multilateral international treaties relating to victims, as defined in paragraph 18.

(21) States should periodically review existing legislation and practice to ensure their responsiveness to changing circumstances, should enact and enforce, if necessary, legislation proscribing acts that constitute serious abuses of political or economic power, as well as promoting policies and mechanism for the prevention of such acts, and should develop and make readily available right and remedies for victims of such acts.

List of Cases

A. Babu Rao *v.* State of A.P. (1996) 1 Crimes 88 (A.P.).
Adamji Umar *v.* State of Bombay, A.I.R. 1952 S.C. 14.
Aminullah *v.* Emperor, A.I.R. 1922 Cal. 191.
Aparent Joseph alias Current Kunju *v.* State of Kerala, A.I.R. 1973 S.C.I.
Arinder Singh Bagga *v.* State of U.P., A.I.R. 1984 S.C. 571.
Aslam Meah *v.* Emperor 9 L.R. 45 Cal. 817.
Balraj *v.* State of U.P., A.I.R. 1995 S.C. 1995.
Bankat *v.* State of Maharashtra (2005) 1 S.C.C. 343.
B. Ramalamma *v.* State of A.P. (1993) 1 Scale 90.
Bhim Singh *v.* State of J. and K., A.I.R. 1986 S.C. 494.
Bhojappa Hanmanthappa Choudannavar *v.* State of Karnataka (2004) 10 S.C.C. 177.
Bodhisattva Gautam *v.* Subhra Chakraborty, A.I.R. 1996 S.C. 922.
Brij Lal *v.* Prem Chand, A.I.R. 1989 S.C. 1661.
Chairman, Railway Board *v.* Mrs. Chandrima Das, A.I.R. 2000 S.C. 988.
Chief Secretary *v.* Student of A.P.A.U. (2005) 12 S.C.C. 448.
Civil Liberties and Human Rights Organisation *v.* G.O.C. (1997) 1 Gau. L.T. 91.
Chorbyn *v.* Ameer Khan, 21 P.R. 1859 Cr.
Christian Community Welfare Council of India *v.* Govt. of Maharashtra (1994) Mah. L.J. 1769.
Crown *v.* Debi Buksh, 25 P.R. 1868 Cr.
D.K. Basu *v.* State of W.B. (1997) 1 S.C.C. 416.
Delhi Democratic Working Women's Forum *v.* Union of India (1995) 1 S.C.C. 14.

Gram Sabha, Lakhanpur Panti *v.* Ram Deo (1993) Cr.L.J. 3277.
Fariduddin *v.* Emperor, A.I.R. 1926 All. 259.
Ghousia Sultana *v.* Mohd. Ghouse Baig, 1996 Cr.L.J. 2973 (A.P.).
Gurusharan Kaur *v.* State of Rajasthan, 1993 Cr.L.J. 2076 (Raj.).
Guruswami *v.* State of Tamil Nadu, A.I.R. 1995 S.C. 1177.
Harikishan *v.* Sukhvinder, A.I.R. 1988 S.C. 2127.
Inder Singh *v.* State of Punjab, A.I.R. 1995 S.C. 1949.
Inderpuri General Store *v.* Union of India, A.I.R. 1992 J. and K. 2.
Jagannath Giri *v.* State of Bihar (1992) Cr.L.J. 648.
J.M. Mohd. Cassim *v.* G.S.J. Sheikh Thamby Shabib, A.I.R. 1940 Rang. 33.
Joshi *v.* State of Kerala, 1996 Cr.L.J. 143 (Ker.).
Kamchi Bala Talukdar *v.* State of Assam (1997) Cr.L.J. 874 (Gau.).
Keshvan Nair *v.* State Insurance Officer, 1971 A.C.J. 219 (Ker.).
Khatri *v.* State of Bihar, A.I.R. 1982 S.C. 928.
Kumarswami Chetty *v.* Kuppuswami, I.L.R. 41 Mad. 685.
Lawyers Forum for Human Rights *v.* State of W.B. (1999) 1 Cal. N.C.N. 485.
M.C.D. *v.* Association of the Victims for Uphaar Tragedy (2005) 9 S.C.C. 586.
Mallappa *v.* Veerabasappa 1978 M.L.J. (Knt.).
Maya Singh *v.* S.H.O., Police Station Sadar Zira (1991) A.C.J. 439.
Minor *v.* Happersett, 88 U.S. 162 (1975).
Mohammad Giasuddin *v.* State of A.P., A.I.R. 1977 S.C. 1926.
Munnal Lal *v.* State of Himachal Pradesh (1992) Cr.L.J. 1558.
Murti Devi *v.* State of Delhi (1998) 9 S.C.C. 604.
Nand Ballabh Pant *v.* State, A.I.R. 1977 S.C. 892.
Narottam Singh *v.* State of Punjab, A.I.R. 1978 S.C. 1452.
Nilabati Behera *v.* State of Orissa, A.I.R. 1993 S.C. 1960.
Palaniapa Gounder *v.* State of Tamil Nadu, A.I.R. 1977 S.C. 1323.
P.U.D.R. *v.* Police Commissioner, Delhi Police Head Quarter (1989) 4 S.C.C. 730.

Postangabon IV. Thokohim *v.* G.O.C. (1997) 7 S.C.C. 725.
Pushpa Gurung *v.* Assistant Director Welfare C.R.P.F. (1988) 86 Cutt. L.T. 319.
P.U.C.L. *v.* Union of India (1997) 3 S.C.C. 433.
P.U.D.R. *v.* State of Bihar, A.I.R. 1987 S.C. 355.
Rajeshwari Pd. *v.* R.B. Gupta, A.I.R. 1961 Pat. 9.
Ram Lubhaya *v.* Jaga Nath, 30 P.L.R. 361.
Ram Pujan Patel *v.* State of U.P. (1973) 2 S.C.C. 456.
Ram Lal *v.* State of J. and K. (1999) 2 S.C.C. 213.
Rattan Singh *v.* State of Punjab (1979) 4 S.C.C. 719.
R. *v.* Inwood, 60 APP. R. 70 (1974).
R. *v.* Thomson Holiday (1974) Q.B. 592.
R. *v.* Mayanard (1983) Crim. L.R. 821.
Rudal Shah *v.* State of Bihar, A.I.R. 1983 S.C. 1086.
R. Gandhi *v.* Union of India, A.I.R. 1989 Mad. 205.
Saheli, A Women's Resources Centre *v.* Commissioner of Police, A.I.R. 1990 S.C. 513.
Sarup Singh *v.* State of Haryana, A.I.R. 1995 S.C. 2452.
Saleh *v.* Emperor, A.I.R. 1932 Sind. 156.
Saraswati Sutradhar *v.* State of Tripura, 1999 Cr.L.J. 117 (Gau.).
Sarwan Singh *v.* State of Punjab, A.I.R. 1978 S.C. 1525.
Seraj Aslam *v.* State of U.P. (1992) Cr.L.J. 2244.
Sebstian M. Hongray *v.* Union of India, A.I.R. 1979 S.C. 1026.
Shah Chandulal Gokuldas *v.* Patel Baldeo Bhai Ranchhoddas, 1980 Cr.L.J. 514.
Sheikh Abdul Gafar Khan *v.* Vasant Raghunath Dhoble (2003) 7 S.C.C. 749.
S.S. Ahulwalia *v.* Union of India, A.I.R. 2001 S.C.1309.
State *v.* Mohd. Akbar, 1999 Cr.L.J. 112 (J. and K.).
State *v.* Gopilal, 1922 Cr.L.J. 749.
State of Karnataka *v.* H.S. Srinivas Iyengar, 1996 Cr.L.J. 3103 (Kent.).
State of Gujarat *v.* Hon'ble High Court of Gujarat (1998) 7 S.C.C. 392.
State of M.P. *v.* Bala (2005) 8 S.C.C.1.
State of U.P. *v.* Virendra Prasad (2004) 9 S.C.C.37.
State of U.P. *v.* Jodh Singh, A.I.R. 1988 S.C. 1822.

State of M.P. *v.* Mangu, 1995 (4) Crimes 818 (M.P.).
State of Haryana *v.* Darshana Devi (1979) 2 S.C.C. 236.
Sube Singh *v.* State of Haryana, 3 S.C.C. 178.
Surendra Nath Mohanty *v.* State of Orissa (1999) 5 S.C.C. 238.
Surendra Babu *v.* State of A.P. (2005) 1 S.C.C. 347.
Surinder Singh *v.* State (1976) 78 P.L.R. 867.
Synder *v.* Massachussetts, 291 U.S. 97 (1934).
Thulik Kall *v.* State of Tamil Nadu, A.I.R. 1973 S.C. 501.
Vinod Kumar *v.* State of Punjab (1996) Cr.L.J. 1037 (P. and H.).
Y. Suresh Babu *v.* State of U.P. (2005) 1 S.C.C. 347.

Bibliography

(A) LIST OF BOOKS

Atiah P., Accidents, Compensation and the Law, Widenfeld and Nicolson, London, 1970.

Barke, J.L.; We are All Victims, Peel Press, London, 1978.

Barnes, H.E. and Teeters, N.K.; New Horizons of Criminology, Prentice Hall, Englewood Cliff, N.J. 1944.

Bentham, Jeremy; The Ratonale of Punishment, Heward, London, 1825.

Bodenheimer, Edgar; Jurisprudence (Second Indian Reprint, 1997).

Chaturvedi, S.K.; Role of Police in Criminal Justice System, D.K. Publishers, New Delhi, 1996.

Das, Bharat B.; Victim in Criminal Justice System (1997), APH Publishing Corporation, New Delhi.

Devasia, V.V.; Human Rights and Victimology, Dutta and Sons, Nagpur.

Doak, Jonation, Victims' Rights, Human Rights and Criminal Justice, Hart Publishing, 2008.

Durkheim, Emile, Rules of Sociological Method.

Emerton, E., Introduction to the History of Middle Age, Boston, 1888.

Garofalo, Raffaele, Criminology, Boston, 1914.

Ghosh, S.K., Torture and Rape in Police Custody, Ashish Publishing House, 1993.

Henting, Hans Von, Punishment: Its Origin, Purposes and Psychology, London (1937).

Hoyle, Carolyn and Young, Richard, New Visions of Crime Victims, Hart Publishing, 2002.

Hurvitz, Stephen and Christiansen, Karlo; Criminology, 1983, London: George.

Johnstone, Gerry, Restorative Justice, Ideas, Values, Debates, 2002.

Kenny, Criminal Law (15th ed.).

Leary, V.O. and Rayne, E., A Study of Conflict Resolution in Criminal Justice, National Council of Crime and Delinquency (1967).

Merryman, John Henry, The Civil Law Tradition, Stanford University Press (1969).

Muller, Max; The Laws of Manu (in) Secred Book of East, Oxford University Press 1886.

Muller, Max; Brihaspati (in) Secred Book of East, Oxford University Press, 1886.

Princep's, Commentary on The Code of Criminal Procedure, 1973 (Revised by Justice K.D. Shahi) 18th ed., Delhi Law House (2001).

Rawls, John, A., Theory of Justice (1971).

Ranjan, V.N., Victimology in India, Allied Publishers, New Delhi, (1981).

Schatfer, Stephen, Victimology: The Victim and His Criminal Reston, Virginia (1977).

Sen Gupta, N.C., The Evolution of Ancient Indian Law, Eastern Law House, Calcutta, 1953.

Sethna, M.J., Society and Criminal, N.M. Tripathi, Bombay, 1969.

Sutherland, E.H. and Cressey, D.R., Principles of Criminology, 1966.

Viano, Emilio (ed.) Victim and Society, Vintage Press, Washington D.C., 1976.

Walker, David M., The Oxford Companion to Law, Clarendon Press, Oxford, 1980.

Zender, Lucia; Victims, The Oxford Handbook of Criminology, Oxford University Press (3rd ed.).

(B) LIST OF ARTICLES

Alphonso, G.M., 'Victim Compensation: A Conceptual Analysis', *Central Law Quarterly*, Vol. II, 1988, p. 459.

Arumugam I. Rao, "Custodial Violence and Deaths: Problems and Prevention, *C.B.I. Bulletin*, December 1994.

Bose, Sukumar, "Victimology and Allied Issues", *Indian Journal of Criminology and Criminalistic*, 2000, Jan.-Dec. 21 (1-3) and 51-61.

Camehon, Bruce J., "Compensation for Victims of Crime: New Zealand Experiment, 12, *Journal of Public Law* (1963), 367-75.

Chaudhary, Baidyanath, "Victim's Right Against Terrorism and the Administration of Criminal Justice", *Criminal Law Journal*, 2002, March, 108, pp. 60-65.

Cohen, E. Irving, "The Integration of Restitution in Probation Services, 34, *Journal of Criminal Law and Criminology* (1994) 315.

Dayal, Keshav, "Custodial Crimes", *Human Rights Year Book*, 2000.

Diaz, S.M., "Comprehensive Victim Assistance—Indian Situation, *Indian Journal of Criminology*, Vol. 15, 1987, p. 79.

Dutta, R.K., "Victimology Needs Due Awareness", *CBI Bulletin*, 1999, Nov. 7, pp. 10-12.

Fletcher, Lawrence P., 'Restitution in Criminal Process: Procedure for Fixing the Offender's Liability, *The Yale Law Journal* (1984).

Kaur, Balvinder, "Torture and Deaths in Police Custody—A Violation of Right to Life", *National Capital Law Journal*, 1997.

Lakshminath, A., "Criminal Justice in India: Primitive to Post Modernism", 48, *J.I.L.I.*, 2006, pp. 26-56.

Mikva, Aber J. 'Victimless Justice, *Journal of Criminal Law and Criminology* (1980), 189-90.

Minhas, S.S. "Death in Custody and Compensation", *Accidents Claims Journal*, 1995 (Dec.)

Noorani, A.G., "Death in Police Custody", *Economical and Political Weekly*, 1982.

Ramaswami, K.; "Custodial Crimes—An Affront to Human Dignity", *Human Rights Yearbook*, 2000.

Raja, L. Soloman, Judicial Attitude on Compensation to

Victims of Crime (in) Devasia, V.V., Human Rights and Victimology, Dutta and Sons, Nagpur, pp. 148-78.

Rao, S.V. Joga, Victims Restitution, *The Lawyer*, June, 1990, p. 17.

Subramanian, S., "Prevention of Death in Police Custody", *CBI Bulletin*, Jan. 1999.

Vibhute, K.I., Book Review of Mundarthi Samaiah, "Law on Compensation to Victims of Crime and Abuse of Power", 46, *J.I.L.I.* (2004), 594.

———, "Victimology: An Indian Perspective", *Cochin University Law Review*, Vol. 14, 1990, p. 153.

———, Compensating Victims of Crime in India—An Appraisal, 32, *J.I.L.I.*, 1990, p. 68.

Wolfgang, Marvin, E. and Singer, Simon I., "Victim Categories of Crime", 69, *Journal of Criminal Law and Criminology*, 1978, p. 379.

(C) LIST OF STATUTES/DOCUMENTS AND REPORTS

- The Constitution of India, 1950.
- The Indian Penal Code, 1860.
- The Code of Criminal Procedure, 1973.
- The Universal Declaration of Human Rights, 1948.
- The International Covenant on Civil and Political Rights, 1966.
- The U.N. Convention Against Torture and Other Cruel Inhuman or Degrading Treatment or Punishment, 1984.
- The U.N. Declaration of Basic Principles of Justice for Victims of Crime and Abuse of Power, 1985.
- 41st Report of the Law Commission of India, Criminal Procedure Code, Govt. of India, Vol. I, 1969.
- 42nd Report of the Law Commission of India, Indian Penal Code, Govt. of India, Ministry of Law, 1971.

Index